**Third
Edition**

# A HANDBOOK

**For Adjunct/Part-Time Faculty
and Teachers of Adults**

**DONALD GREIVE, Ed.D.**

**Info-Tec, Inc.**

**To Order:**

**Info-Tec, Inc.**
**1005 North Abbe Road**
**Elyria, OH 44035-1691**
**1-800-995-5222 x4632**
**Fax: 1-216-365-6519**


Third Printing: June 1996


© 1995, 1990, 1984 by Info-Tec, Inc.

**Library of Congress Data**
Catalog Card Number: 95-079487
ISBN 0-940017-22-9 (P)
ISBN 0-940017-21-0 (C)

Printed in the United States of America

# Preface

Increasing numbers of adult students in all types of educational institutions are being taught by part-time faculty. Thus, the role of part-time/adjunct faculty will continue to take on additional importance. The professional development of adjunct faculty is an integral part in the success of institutions. Often, part-time faculty, who have other jobs or responsibilities, do not have time to adequately develop techniques and strategies for successful classroom teaching.

This publication is intended to help remedy that situation. *A Handbook for Adjunct/Part-Time Faculty and Teachers of Adults* is written for practitioner's who have the need but not the time for formal in-depth coursework in professional enhancement. Although protected by copyright, it is the intent of the author that faculty receive the greatest support from its contents. Therefore, faculty are granted permission to reproduce for personal use any of the forms herein that have a direct application to their teaching endeavors.

Donald Greive, Ed. D.

# Contents

## *Chapter 4*

# Teaching Adult Students ............................................. 49

*Chapter 5*

# Some Practical Teaching Suggestions —From Teachers ...... 63

# Acknowledgments

It is difficult with a growing and living publication such as this to adequately recognize all of the individuals who have provided valuable input. To those people, too numerous to name, who have suggested changes and additions through conversation and informal communication, thank you—your observations were taken seriously and greatly appreciated.

There are also several individuals whose contributions were paramount to the completion of this publication. For their significant efforts in the evaluation of the previous edition of *The Handbook* and for their in-depth suggestions, I am indebted to Robert Dolan, City University; Anita C. R. Gorham, Central Michigan University; Michael Parsons, Hagerstown Junior College; Harry Schuler, Chapman University, and Gary Wheeler, Miami University. With their important special topic contributions, Richard Clemens, Wright State University; Dennis Gabriel, Cuyahoga Community College; Jaslin Salmon, Triton College; and Arlene Sego provided input of great value to the content of the book. And for the monumental task of editing and typesetting the document, I am forever grateful to Ann Devaty Kiraly and Deb Loukota-Durkee. To Mickey Sego, I owe the cover design and many years of encouragement in the publication of books and materials for colleges and universities.

Many individuals submitted manuscripts for chapter five, I am especially grateful for your efforts. Although space limitations did not permit the inclusion of all manuscripts, the authors of those used are included with the text. Finally, without the support, encouragement, and input from Janet and Jerry, this publication would not have happened.

Don Greive

# Teaching: What It's All About

## Orientation to College and Adult Teaching

In the coming decades, teachers of college and adult students will be faced with many challenges that did not previously exist. Compared to the classroom of 15-20 years ago, the evolution is complete to the modern classroom of the 21st century. The influx of a multi-cultural and multi-lingual student body, the impact of technology, and the increasing numbers of students with varying abilities attending college, have caught the attention of educators everywhere. In addition, the changing economic and political pressures throughout the world have impacted education and, you, the instructor.

Whether you are teaching in a continuing education program of business, industry or the military; in a liberal arts college with tradition, values, and campus ministry; in a community college where the role is to serve as an open door institution; in a public university with its research and graduate school emphasis, or in an adult education center, you will feel the impact. The students of today will be more highly motivated, more challenging and in many ways more enjoyable to teach.

With the concern for accountability and the realization that there are established strategies and techniques for instruction, there is greater emphasis upon improved teaching. The rise of the project technique in business and industry has provided impetus for its adoption by the educational community. Adult students employed in business and industry expect a planned and organized classroom. It is no longer a question of whether there are going to be instructional objectives and strategies for teaching; it is a question of how skilled instructors are in developing and delivering them.

Already we are seeing signs of classrooms being equipped with computers. Projection devices are not uncommon. Many institutions have overhead projectors in every classroom. Video tape and television are common and rarely do we see a movie projector. Not only will modern faculty need to understand this transition and cope with it, but often they will be required to utilize the technology as another activity in the motivation of students.

These factors, however, do not minimize the human element of teaching. If you enjoy being a teacher, there is nothing wrong with telling the students that you are there because you enjoy teaching. Being cheerful, open, and understanding is always an asset to good teaching. Students will like to hear your experiential anecdotes; share them. Look upon the class as a project. Adult students expect planning and preparation and will not rebel if it is required. Be aware of your cultural and intellectual environment. Strive to be a good and successful instructor and your teaching experiences will be exciting, rewarding, and satisfying.

It might be good for you to take a few moments before your first class to meditate about your purpose for teaching. This will do two things: it will encourage you to more clearly identify your role and personal goals and objectives, and it will increase your confidence. There may be students who question why someone with your expertise would spend their time teaching a college course. Be prepared. Have a few answers ready if students ask. If they don't ask, you might want to include it as a part of your personal introduction. You certainly have good reasons. It might be to your advantage to communicate them. The facts that you just enjoy teaching, like interaction with others, like the stimulation, enjoy being in front of a group, feel it improves your skills, and many other reasons you might identify are appropriate.

A commonly accepted axiom in education is that learning is

best accomplished when there is a need for the learning and when it is built upon former learning and knowledge. *From these observations we can conclude that most learning, contrary to popular belief, is not the responsibility of teachers. It is the responsibility of learners.* Faculty as facilitators, however, can utilize the above principles to ease the learning tasks of students. The ideal situation, of course, is one in which both the need for learning and former knowledge are in proper perspective. Learning starts with the knowledge and skills that students bring with them to class and not necessarily the content knowledge brought by faculty. Teaching is still a vocation, a calling, if you will, to individuals who enjoy being with people and feel intrinsic satisfaction in helping others and themselves to grow.

## Characteristics of Good Teaching

Using one's mind in the pursuit of knowledge and at the same time sharing it with fellow citizens is in itself gratifying. The responsibility for a class and potential influence upon students are very stimulating. It remains stimulating, however, only so long as the instructor continues to grow and remain dynamic. The qualities of good teaching are quite simple:

* Knowing your subject content.
* Knowing and liking students.
* Understanding our culture.
* Possessing command of professional teaching skills and strategies.

Knowing your subject content means simply that you have a command of your discipline and the capability of calling upon resources. Knowing students is part of the teaching process and is aided by formal and informal communication within and outside the classroom. Understanding our culture has become more complex for todays' instructor. Sensitivity to the diverse cultures in your classroom is necessary to success in teaching. Finally, it is necessary that college teachers continue to develop and improve strategies and techniques for the delivery of instruction in the classroom.

Some characteristics that students look for in good teachers are:

1. Being knowledgeable, organized, and in control.
2. Possesses good communication skills and utilizes techniques to enhance classroom communication.
3. Having a good attitude and empathy, and exhibits honesty.
4. Being fair in treatment of individuals in class, as well as in evaluation.
5. Being professional and business-like appearance and conduct.
6. Utilizing questions and other techniques to stimulate discussion and involve students.
7. Having a pleasant personality.
8. Utilizing a variety of teaching techniques and strategies.
9. Taking time for individual students and their concerns.
10. Striving to build student self-esteem and success.

## The First Class

As you prepare for your first class, considerable anxiety and nervousness will be experienced. This has always been true of teaching and will continue to be true in the future. In fact, many experienced teachers feel they do their best work if they are slightly nervous and anxious. Excessive nervousness and anxiety, however, can be a distraction to the teaching-learning process and efforts should be made to minimize them.

In preparation for the first class, keep in mind that it is nearly impossible to prepare for all situations. The speed at which the class presentation will go cannot be anticipated. Many times student response is significantly greater or less than expected. Having excessive material prepared for the first class will ally this problem and is worth the extra effort in confidence gained.

Another major factor in facing the first class is knowing yourself as a teacher. Anyone mature enough to be teaching has some feeling of his/her own personal characteristics. Most of us are average in appearance; however, we usually have gone through life compensating for variations from the average. There is no more need to be self-conscious in front of a class than there is in any social situation. Minor compensations may be necessary. If you have a tendency toward casual or even sloppy appearance, appearing neat and professional will pay off. If you have a light voice, practice in expression may be well worth the time spent. Generally speaking, part of the student size-up will include your appearance and actions. If you are timid-take charge. Being in control pays off not only in eliminating barriers to classroom communication, but in developing self-confidence in teaching.

Remember, students are not solely impressed by the knowledge and experience of the teacher; they are equally influenced by related factors. Some guidelines for the first class are:

*   Plan an activity that allows students to get involved immediately. It may simply be an information gathering format.
*   Initiate casual conversation between yourself and students and among the students prior to presenting the specifics of the course.
*   Make certain you are early, at least 20 minutes before the start of class. If possible, greet your students.
*   Present on an overhead or handout your course objectives and goals.
*   Identify course standards including time required for outside work.
*   Use an icebreaker, if possible a question that is related to your course but does not have a specific answer.
*   Take care of housekeeping items such as breaks and restroom locations.
*   Conduct a class—don't meet and dismiss. First impressions are lasting.

Some successful instructors begin their first class by asking students to write a short paragraph about themselves and their concerns. Often students are willing to discuss their anxieties. This will help in understanding the class.

## Setting the Tone

Professional educators and teacher trainers agree that creating positive feelings about the course is an important goal of the instructor. Often instructors assume that students are aware of the fact that they intend to be pleasant, cooperative, and helpful. However, this should not be taken for granted. With differing personalities and types of students in the classroom, faculty members must realize that a positive comment or gesture to one student may in fact be negative to another student. Thus, faculty should make a concerted effort to show pleasantness in their behavior. A smile, a pleasant comment, or a laugh with students who are attempting to be funny will pay great dividends.

In setting the tone of the classroom, permissiveness is sometimes a good strategy. We are all familiar with traditional teaching in which students were essentially "passive" learners. We are also familiar with situations where excessive permissiveness was a distraction to other students. Teachers of adults must be cognizant of the fact that flexibility and permissiveness are important to a proper learning environment, and that encouraging creativity and unexpected comments is part of the learning and teaching process. Excessive distraction can always be controlled. The instructor has ultimate authority and need not exercise it to prove it for its own sake. Remember, permissiveness and flexibility require considerable working skill. Authority is there with the role.

## Teachers Are Actors/Actresses

In reality, teachers are on stage; they are actors or actresses whether or not they recognize and admit it. A teacher in front of the classroom carries all of the responsibility and requires all of the talent of anyone on stage or taking part in a performance. Due to modern technology, unfortunately, students compare faculty to professionals they have seen in other roles. Thus, adjunct faculty must be alert to the ramifications.

Faculty members have within themselves all of the emotions of stage performers with greater audience interaction. There may be, on occasion, an emotional reaction and you should prepare for it. As an instructor, you will experience fear, joy, and feelings of tentativeness, but also feelings of extreme confidence and satisfaction. Handle fear with good preparation; confidence brought forward with good preparation is the easiest way to allay fear. Remove anxieties from the classroom by developing communication systems. Some adjunct faculty members are effective at using humor. As a general rule, however, humor should be used delicately. Jokes are completely out. Almost any joke that is told will offend someone.

## Classroom Communication

Many kinds of communication exist in every classroom situation. You must be aware that facial expressions, and eye contact with students, as well as student interaction, are all forms of communication.

A major goal is to ascertain that classroom communication is structured in a positive manner. Communication starts the moment you enter the classroom on the first day or evening of class. As is indicated elsewhere in this publication, the method by which you commence the first class and the initial interaction with students is indicative of the type of communication that will exist throughout the course. The amount of student participation as the course progresses is an indicator of the direction in which the communication is flowing. Since many students today are adults, there is greater opportunity to call upon their experiences. The discussion of facts, events, examples, analogies, and anecdotes will often elicit an association with your adult students. This will encourage students to share experiences and anecdotes of their own. The best communication device still is verbal.

Some specific activities (described in detail in chapter 3) that can be used include: use of open-ended questions, critical thinking techniques, anecdotes, and class problem solving activities. Activities involving students include: buzz groups, the partner system, panels, collaborative learning, student reports, brainstorming and group discussion. Remember, a good class is dynamic, communicative, participative, and interactive.

## The Three R's of Teaching

Much has been written about the three R's of learning. The three R's of teaching, however, are equally important.

The three R's of good teaching are: repeat, respond, and reinforce. Very simply, they mean student comments and contributions, if worthy of being recognized in class, are worthy of being repeated. A simple repeat, however, is not sufficient. You should elicit an additional response either from the class or the student making the original statement. After the response, reinforcement of the statement or conclusions should be stated. These three simple rules improve class relationships by emphasizing the importance of the students, the students to each other, and their contributions. They promote two way communication and represent application of one of the basic tenants of learning . . . reinforcement.

## Teaching Styles

Just as students have styles of learning, it is appropriate that part-time faculty members recognize their own styles of teaching. In relation to students who view themselves as consumers, as well as learners, the style that the teacher brings to the classroom is important. For example, an instructor who emphasizes facts in teaching will find difficulty in developing meaningful discussions with students who have progressed to the analysis stage of their learning. It is not important that part-time instructors modify their behavior to match that of students. It is important, however, that part-time faculty recognize their own teaching styles and adapt teaching processes, techniques, and strategies to enhance their most effective style. Some questions in assisting in the self-determination of teaching styles are:

1. Do I tend to be authoritative, directional, semi-directional, or laissez-faire in my classroom leadership?

2. Do I solicit communication with and between students easily or with difficulty?

3. Am I well-organized and well-planned?

4. Am I meticulous in my appearance as a professional, or

do I have a tendency to put other priorities first and show up in class as is?

I have found that teaching styles, as many of life's other ventures, are not static. Many of the techniques used early in my career with younger students who appreciated humor and diversion were not as effective later with more mature students who felt they were there to learn, not to be entertained. I noticed later in my career that although I was well-organized, had well stated objectives, used good class communication, and observed the characteristics that I deemed important to good teaching, I had become too serious. For that reason I now occasionally mix in with my lesson plan an additional sheet that says to me "smile, be friendly, smell the roses."

Also, I found an evolution in the use of anecdotes. Strangely enough it was the reverse. Early in my career the use of anecdotes sometimes drew criticism from students as "too much story telling," or "more war stories." Later I began to put the question on my evaluation questionnaires: "Were the anecdotes and stories meaningful?" The overwhelming response from adult students was "yes." They were meaningful, they brought meaning to the class, and they were valuable because the adults were interested to know of experiences from people who were actually practitioners. One note of caution, the use of anecdotes should relate to the topic being discussed and not simply be stories of other experiences. In general, however, it can be concluded that most of today's students approve of anecdotes . . . *and may have their own to contribute.*

## The Diverse Classroom

Since 1970, the United States has experienced a dramatic increase in the number and proportion of minorities and women attending college. It is expected that the racial and cultural diversity of institutions of higher education will continue to increase; as this occurs, it becomes incumbent on college teachers to ensure that their approach to teaching demonstrates that they value racial and cultural diversity. Specific steps must be taken to enhance relationships with students who are racially or culturally different. Salmon (1994) provides the following specific suggestions about things to avoid as well as constructive behaviors:

1. Under no circumstances should a student be given a "preferred name." Learn to pronounce **all** names.
2. Do not assume that a minority student knows a lot about his or her group.
3. Even if no member of a particular group is in a class, avoid talking negatively about the group.
4. Do not tell or tolerate racist, sexist, ethnic, or age related jokes.
5. When alluding to racial and cultural differences, do not imply a negative.
6. Do not leave the impression that all blacks live in ghettos, that all Hispanics are illegal aliens, that all native Americans are drunkards or that all women are money grabbers.
7. Avoid the use of stereotypical characterizations of **any** group.

**Constructive Behaviors:**

1. The professor must become aware of his or her own prejudices.
2. The professor must not use his or her personal values as the sole basis for judging students.
3. The faculty member must become knowledgeable about those he or she serves.
4. The educator must constantly evaluate his or her perceptions to ensure that they are not based on personal insecurities.
5. Every effort must be made to ensure that the information one has is a reliable basis for judgment.

*"The Diverse Classroom" contributed by Jaslin Salmon, Ph. D., Triton College, River Grove, IL. For complete discussion see Chapter 3, "Teaching in Racially and Culturally Diverse Environments",* **TEACHING IN COLLEGE-A RESOURCE FOR COLLEGE TEACHERS,** *referenced in bibliography. Jaslin Salmon provides consultant services for diversity programs.*

## Professional Ethics

Although the teaching profession has been slow (compared to other professions) in addressing ethical issues, developments of the past few decades have required an examination of the ethical expectations of college faculty. Although the present situation has been brought about mainly by legal or public relations concerns, there has always existed an unwritten set of ethics for teachers based upon a set of values that have evolved both within the teaching profession and our culture. As Wilbert McKeachie states, "Ethical standards are intended to guide us in carrying out the responsibilities we have to the different groups with whom we interact" (McKeachie, 1994). Some institutions have adopted written standards of ethical behavior expected of all college faculty. A summary of such standards is listed below. This summary has been compiled as a guideline for individual part-time faculty and is not intended to represent a legal position in relation to the faculty member and his/her host institution. For clarity, the guidelines are presented in two categories: those pertaining to the profession of teaching, and those pertaining to students.

**Ethics and the Profession.** This section is an attempt to emphasize the ethical expectations of the profession and the institution in which part-time faculty are employed. Adjunct faculty:

1. Will attend all classes assigned with adequate preparation of materials and content as described in the course description.
2. Will not attempt to teach a course for which they are not qualified and knowledgeable.
3. On controversial issues, will present all sides of the issue.
4. Will conduct a fair evaluation of students applied equally to all.
5. Will not promote outside entrepreneurial activities within the class setting.
6. When reasonably possible, attend college orientations and other development activities presented for the improvement of their role as an instructor.

7. Will avoid behavior that may be interpreted as discriminatory based upon gender, age, social status or ethnic background.

8. Will hold their colleagues and institution in highest respect in their actions and communication within and outside the institution.

**Professional Ethics and Students.** This section relates to ethical considerations concerning students. Adjunct faculty:

1. Will not discuss individual students and their problems outside of the professional structure of the institution.

2. Will refer personal problems of students to qualified staff.

3. Will maintain and honor office hours or appointments with students.

4. Will respect students integrity and avoid social encounters with students which might suggest misuse of power.

5. Will not attempt to influence students' philosophy or their position concerning social and political issues.

6. Will not ask students for personal information for research data.

These guidelines are quite general, however they may provide a vehicle for discussion to examine more closely the expectations of the institution in which you teach. Unfortunately, in today's world, there is sometimes a fine line between an ethical issue and a legal issue.

## Andragogy and Pedagogy

It is entirely possible that you may be employed as an adjunct faculty member in an institution that has an established development program. In faculty development workshops, you might encounter the theory of andragogy. This section will attempt to clarify for you the concepts of andragogy and pedagogy.

Most of us, as both learners and teachers, are familiar with the educational process of pedagogy which assumes that the instructor has the responsibility to determine what is to be learned and how it will be learned. Much of our class planning is centered around this concept and is driven by the needs of the academic discipline.

Andragogy on the other hand, according to Knowles, is based on several assumptions that may not fit the pedagogical model. They are: adults need to know why they need to learn something; adults are responsible for their own decisions; adults come with a greater volume and different quality of experience; adults come ready to learn those things they need to know and adult learning is life centered, not subject centered (Knowles, 1990).

The purpose of this section is not to favor one concept over the other, but to inform you as a faculty member of the existence of the debate. However, you will find that many of the instructional strategies described in this book utilize the concept of andragogy as well as pedagogy.

## TQM and CQI

Total Quality Management and Continuous Quality Improvement are two management/delivery systems that may effect you if your institution is involved in the processes. TQM, the management system popularized in industry by Deming, involves participator management by all individuals in the organization. The system attempts improvement through empowering not only the instructor, but students as well, to determine goals (objectives), methods (andragogy-pedagogy), and evaluation (outcomes). It is a team-centered concept in which you may be requested to participate.

Continuous Quality Improvement (CQI) involves problem solving teams to examine identified problems and focus on their correction. This process normally develops teams of six to eight people. Both of these processes view students as a customer/worker.

## Checklist for Part-Time Faculty

There are many things that you need to know when receiving your teaching assignment. Each teaching situation may call for new information. There are, however, basic items that will almost assuredly be asked at sometime during class. This section lists several items that you may wish to check before entering the first class.

After reviewing this list, it is recommended that a personal timeline be developed including these and other important dates related to teaching the course.

## Faculty Checklist

1. What are the names of the department chairperson, dean, director and other officials?
2. Have I completed all of my paperwork for official employment? (It's demoralizing when an expected paycheck doesn't arrive.)
3. Is there a pre-term faculty meeting?
   Date_____ Time_____
4. Is there a departmental course syllabus, course outline, or statement of goals and objectives available for the course?
5. Are there prepared departmental handouts?
6. Are there prepared departmental tests?
7. Where is and how do I get my copy of the text and support materials for teaching the class?
8. Is there a department and/or college attendance or tardiness policy?
9. When are grades due? When do students receive grades?
10. Is there a college or departmental grading policy?
11. Where can I get instructional aid materials and equipment, films, video tapes, software, and what is the lead time for ordering?
12. Is there a student evaluation of instruction in this course? Do I have a sample copy?

# Planning

There are many suggestions for good teaching discussed in this publication, however, the most important activity for part-time faculty is planning. Planning is essential to a successful teaching situation. Many of the students in your class come from a structured background or employment situations where plans and performance objectives are required. Also, over the past several years, planning has taken on added importance because of the legal implications for institutions concerning product advertisement. The best protection for this kind of action is for instructors to have a written, viable plan.

Good planning requires a comprehensive approach, beginning with the course description and ending with the students' evaluation. Executing the plan is much like a football game; nearly everyone knows the standard plays and the standard procedures; the execution is what determines the winner.

Planning must take place prior to the first class. The preliminary steps include textbook familiarization, organization of the material into content areas and topics, and ranking goals and objectives. An assignment of class time for each of the major topics and a plan for a number of activities for each also is needed. In addition, develop "fillers" for class sessions when you need additional material. Good planning includes several documents. They include:

1. The lesson plan
2. The course outline
3. The course syllabus

4. Course objectives
5. An evaluation plan

## The Lesson Plan

The lesson plan is a must for all teachers. It acts as a reference and guide for each class meeting. It contains the main topics for each lesson. Flexible lesson plans allow discussion of appropriate current events. The flexible lesson plan supports media activities and provides a backup system if materials or equipment do not arrive or if there is a mechanical or electrical malfunction. The plan contains key questions and quotes from supplemental material not contained in the text. It includes definitions, comments on purposes of the class, student activities, and teacher activities.

Make every effort to have lesson plans reflect your creative endeavors and unique abilities a teacher. Often, the syllabus and to some extent the course outline are dictated to faculty. The demands for accountability and the goals of the institution restrict and limit the flexibility of these two documents. Lesson plans, however, allow the greatest opportunity for flexibility and permit techniques and strategies unique to the instructor. You may include appropriate personal experiences and anecdotes in the lesson plan. Shown in figures 1 and 2 are examples of a lesson plan and a sample form. An effective method of planning a course is to construct a plan for each class meeting, number the lessons, place them in a loose leaf binder, and maintain them as a record and a guide for activities.

Figure 1

---

**Sample Lesson Plan**

Course # and Name: Algebra 101

Date_____

Session #9

Class Objectives:
  1. To demonstrate equations through the use of various expressions of equality
  2. To prove equality of expressions through technique of substitution

Definitions:
1. Equation is a statement that two expressions are equal
2. Expression is a mathematical statement
3. Linear equation is equation of 1st order

Student Activities:
1. Complete sample problems in class
2. Demonstrate competence of sample by board work

Instructor Activities:
1. Demonstrate validity of solution of equations
2. Assure student understanding by personal observations by seat and board work

Major Impact:
Understand the solution of basic linear equations.
Assignment: Problems—Exercise 8, pp. 41-42.

---

Figure 2

---

### Suggested Lesson Plan Format

Course number and name _____
*(after first page simply number chronologically)*

Date _____

Session # _____

Definitions to be covered _____

_____

Class objective(s) _____

_____

Student activities or exercises _____

_____

Instructor activities _____

_____

Major impact or thought _____

_____

Assignment _____

_____

## The Course Outline

While the lesson plan is a daily map to ensure direction and activity for the session, the course outline is much more comprehensive and allows you to monitor the map of the entire course.

The course outline is usually a formal document. Use the standard outline format to cover the topics in detail. Generally, a topic need not be divided into more than three subtopics for a class outline. If there are more than three subtopics, place them in the daily class lesson plan. The purpose of the outline is very simple: to make certain that all major topics are recognized and addressed during the course.

The two types of outlines most commonly used in teaching are the **chronological outline** and the **content outline.** Content outlines are used with topics taught in a specified content order. It is often called a topical outline. The chronological outline is used for courses which lend themselves to time and historic sequence.

Sequential courses, such as mathematics, history and science, where previous knowledge is necessary to function at a higher level, are chronological outlines. Content outlines allow considerable flexibility. Faculty arrange the course in a way that is most effective for presentation. For example, physical education faculty may allow students to actually perform an activity prior to its being taught so that the students can see a need for the techniques. Whereas, a chronological outline calls for the presentation of the basic information before students attempt to perform the operation. A course concerned with legislative, judicial, or community activities, would not require that field trips to legislative bodies or courtrooms be conducted in sequence with other activities in the course.

Although in most institutions there are course outlines available, generally they will not be maintained as formal documents. Often, outlines are treated in the same manner as lesson plans, that is, something to be developed by the instructor. (The formal document recognized at most institutions and approved by the college is the course syllabus). A sample course outline is shown in figure 3. Theoretically, a proper course outline is developed in direct relationship to the course objectives.

This assures direction and purpose of the outline.

---

Figure 3

---

**Sample Course Outline**

**Basic Statistics 101**

**I. Introduction**
    A. Basic statistics-use and purposes
    B. Data gathering
        1. Instruments
        2. Recorded data
        3. Machine utilization

**II. Presenting Data**
    A. Tables
        1. Summary tables
            a. Table elements
            b. Tables with averages
    B. Graphs
        1. Types of graphs
            a. Bar
            b. Pie chart
            c. Line graph
        2. Data presentation with graphs
    C. Frequency distributions
        1. Discrete and continuous
        2. Class intervals

**III. Descriptions and Comparison of Distributions**
    A. Percentiles
        1. Computation of percentile
        2. Inter-percentile range
        3. Percentile score
    B. Mean and standard deviations
        1. Computation of mean
            a. From grouped data
            b. From arbitrary origin
        2. Variance formulas
    C. Frequency distributions
        1. Measures of central tendency
        2. Symmetry and skewness
        3. Bimodal distributions

**IV. Predictive or Estimative Techniques**
   A. Regression
      1. Graphic application
      2. Assumptions of linearity
   B. Correlation
      1. Computation of correlation coefficient
      2. Reliability of measurement
   C. Circumstances affecting regression and analysis
      1. Errors of measurement
      2. Effect of range
      3. Interpretation of size
**V. The Normal Curve and Statistical Inference**
   A. The normal distribution
      1. Mean
      2. Standard deviation
      3. Characteristics
   B. Statistical inference
      1. Employing samples
         a. Randomness
         b. Parameters
      2. Normal Distribution
         a. Standard errors
         b. Unbiased estimate
         c. Confidence interval
   C. Testing hypothesis
      1. Definition of statistical hypothesis
      2. Test of hypothesis
         a. Level of significance
         b. One-sided test
      3. Computing power of test

# The Course Syllabus

A syllabus is defined in the dictionary as *"a concise statement of the main points of a course of study or subject."* Although this definition leaves room for interpretation (what constitutes "concise"? and what constitutes "the main points"?), one thing is certain:  The syllabus is the official document of the course. The syllabus is the document that should be shared with students and filed as a permanent contribution to the instructional archives of the college. Thus, it is probably the most important document in the educational process.

The reason there is confusion in academia concerning syllabi is that faculty members may interpret the word syllabus differently. For example, a concise statement to one faculty member may simply mean "Chapter V," whereas to another faculty member the concise statement may mean enumerating the major points of Chapter V, describing each point, and writing a complete sentence for each. Even though the syllabus is one of the most important documents in education, part-time faculty probably will encounter situations where such a document is not available. There are two reasons for this:

1.  Course development and presentation have been left completely to the wishes of individual faculty member and faculty are not required to make it available to institutional sources.
2.  Part-time faculty may be teaching a new or recently revised course for which a syllabus has not been developed.

Development of the syllabus is a multi-step process. A good syllabus has several major parts:

1.  The complete name of the course, including the course   number and catalog description
2.  The name and title by which the faculty member wishes to be addressed
3.  The faculty members' office hours
4.  The text or texts and outside readings required
5.  The course requirements and grading standards
6.  The course objectives
7.  The assignments and  projects to be completed by the   students
8.  A complete listing of resources, outside readings, field  trips
9.  The evaluation plan

**Objectives.** The first major part of the syllabus is the listing of the course objectives. Listing the objectives for a course is often difficult for new faculty members. The tendency is to make certain that everything of importance in the course is included. This dilutes the purpose of the objectives and makes them less valuable to the teaching process. As a general rule, most courses can be adequately described by developing not more than ten to fourteen objectives. *One must be certain, however, that the objectives are reachable, they are teachable, and student learning activities can be directed to each.* This activity is covered in greater detail later in this chapter.

**Student Activities.** Following the course objectives, the syllabus describes the activities of the students that will result in their meeting the course requirements. This should include detailed specific activities, such as outside reading, laboratory activities, projects, and assignments. Describe these activities in a way that relates directly to the objectives. Significant attention should be given to the reasons for the activities and how they relate to the course. This approach tells students that the class is all business and that there is a purpose for everything.

**Course Requirements.** Next, the syllabus should include a detailed description of the course requirements as well as student responsibilities. This is one of the most important parts of the syllabus because it defines for students exactly what is expected. It eliminates the possibility that students will claim ignorance of what was expected. In fact, it is useful in this section of the syllabus to list the class meetings by day and date, the reading and homework assignments and other activities and class topics to be addressed. Many experienced faculty members have felt that all this detail was not necessary until they found themselves in an indefensible position concerning student accusations that the course content was not adequately covered. Sometimes this section of the syllabus is broken into two or more parts; however, the general rule is that excessive detail is better than too little detail.

**Resources and References.** Finally, the syllabus should include a complete listing of resources, outside readings, bibliographies, and visitations to which the student may wish to refer. Without fail, required outside readings and library reserve assignments should be specified. Again, excessive detail is of value. One need not be concerned if the syllabus eventually grows into a document of five pages or more. The students will be appreciative of the faculty member's efforts, and the instructor will be adequately protected in the event evidence of course content or teacher preparation is needed.

Distribute the syllabus the first day of class and take time to discuss the syllabus and anecdotal details. In fact, it is good practice to review the syllabus on the second class meeting and note the importance of the activities, assignments and objectives. The importance of the syllabus to students can best be exemplified by a recent experience of the author while teaching a summer class. Before the second class session I was approached by a student, who had missed the first session, with a request for a copy of my syllabus and course outline. A sign of the rising expectations of students.

A good syllabus requires considerable work initially but minimal time in subsequent updates. Work put into the development of the syllabus will pay dividends. A syllabus is a scientific document and a work of art, and it should be shown that respect in its development and use. Figure 4 is a sample of a completed syllabus:

Figure 4

## Achievement University
### Syllabus

Name of Course:   English 101-33241

Instructor:   Dr. Dennis

Office:   B151

Phone:   987-5037 (0ffice)
dgabrie@ibm5060.ccc.edu (Internet address)
fax 987-5050

Office Hours:   M-F 9:00 to 10:00
M, W, F, 12:00 to 2:00 (by appointment)

Lecture hours:   3

Lab hours:   0

Class requirements:

> All papers must be typed or written on a word processor. Papers may be revised for a higher grade.Use the MLA format for all papers. Plan to spend three to four hours each week in the computer lab.

Course description (per catalog):     Study and practice in the principles of good writing.

Performance objectives:

1. The student will organize and clarify the principles of basic written communication.
2. The student will complete critical readings as a basis for completion of his/her writing.
3. The student will develop and increase skills in expository and argumentative writing.

> Essay patterns:
>
> > Narrative
> > Expository (analysis, contrast, cause-effect)
> > Argument

Schedule:

January
10     Introduction to the course
       Diagnostic essay
       Homework: read Chs. 1, 2, (handbook)

17     Discuss essay patterns, Ch. 2
       Return diagnostic essay w/comments
       Discuss essay 1: narrative
       Hmwk: read Ch. 3

24     Discuss subordination, Ch. 3
       Discuss variety and details, Ch. 3
       Assign essay 2
       Essay 1 due
       Hmwk: Ch. 4

31     Discuss Ch. 4 writing the introduction, conclusion
       Crash course in phonicsPunctuation (handout)
       Discuss essay 2
       Hmwk: Ch. 5

February
7      Subject and verb agreement
      Usage problems
      Essay 2 due
      Hmwk: Ch. 6
14     Support paragraphs
      Developing topics
      Assign essay 3
      Hmwk: Ch. 7
21     Using the exact word
      Punctuation problems
      Essay 3 due
28     Pronoun and antecedent
      Usage problems
      Assign essay 4
      Hmwk: Ch. 9

March
7      Writing a paper for a literature class
      Essay 4 due
      Writing across the curriculum
      Hmwk: Ch. 10
14     Discuss topic for final exam
      Review course goals, objectives
      Hmwk: Outline final exam

Textbooks:    **The Compact Handbook**
               **American Heritage Dictionary, 3e**

Supplemental materials:  3.5 disk, HD

Suggested daily/weekly readings:    **New York Times**
                                      **Newsweek** magazine
                                      **Wall Street Journal**

Last day to drop class:  4 March
Attendance policy:  Attendance in class is important. To that end, quizzes may NOT be made up.
Final grade:  Quizzes         20% (one per week)
             Essay 1         10% (due 1/24)
             Essay 2         20% (due 2/7)
             Essay 3         20% (due 2/21)
             Essay 4         10% (due 3/7)
             Final exam     20% (2/21, 8 to 10 AM)

## Writing Objectives

The development of appropriate course objectives has become commonplace. No longer is there dialogue whether or not college courses will have objectives; all courses and classes must have objectives. The success of faculty depends to a great extent upon their ability to develop and implement course objectives. A brief flowchart shown below indicates the major components of the teaching/planning process.

The most important activity in this process is that of developing appropriate course objectives.

Fortunately, the development of good course objectives is not as complex and difficult as we were previously led to believe. There do exist, however, two remaining pitfalls: (1) The tendency to write more objectives than can be covered in class. (2) The tendency to write objectives that are not clear to the student. There are two very simple techniques to overcome these problems.

First, in order to avoid writing objectives in a haphazard manner, simply develop the course goals and write the objectives for the goals rather than for the course. Course goals are easily identified; they are developed from the catalog course description. Once you have written the goals, write the objectives to support the goals. Don't worry about the ramifications of low priority objectives. A simple format to use for this is to take a blank sheet of paper and put one goal on each sheet of paper. Then construct the objectives that will be implemented for each goal.

The second part of the process, clarity of understanding, can most easily be addressed by clearly identifying the descriptors to be used in writing the objectives. Descriptors should be few but concise. Developing appropriate objectives is merely verbalizing and writing your thoughts concerning the objective. After the statement has been verbalized, apply the appropriate descriptors:

| | |
|---|---|
| write | solve |
| contrast | compare |

| | |
|---|---|
| compose | describe |
| recite | construct |
| compute | identify |
| list | attend |

When writing objectives, remember that you must measure whether or not the objective has been reached.

Conversely, descriptors that should not be used since they cannot be clearly measured for completion include:

| | |
|---|---|
| understand | appreciate |
| enjoy | believe |
| grasp | |

It is not necessary to have conditional lead-ins, such as "at the completion of . . ."; that is understood. Some conditions may be included, for example, the achievement of a certain rating score or the achievement of a certain activity in a given time. Make every effort, however, to be clear in terms of student understanding of the conditions. Good objectives are essential to a good planning process. ***You should evaluate and assign grades on the basis of the completion of the course objectives.*** Robert Mager, one of the pioneers of the instructional objective movement, outlines several principles to be observed in writing objectives (Mager, 1962): a. be explicit, b. communicate, c. tell what the learner will be doing, d. indicate conditions if there are any, e. include some recognition of it being achieved.

Examples of some well written objectives are:

1.  The student will recite the Gettysburg Address.
2.  The student will identify the major components of a successful lesson plan.
3.  The student will describe the process involved in a bank approval of a consumer loan.
4.  The student will write a five-page news release on a selected, identified topic with a minimum of two errors.

## Faculty Self-Evaluation

Many colleges today have forms available for faculty who wish to conduct self-evaluations. If used, whether voluntary or mandatory, keep in mind that most of these forms are in fact student opionnaires and not statistically valid instruments.

This does not, however, decrease the value of faculty's seeking student input to improve teaching. Whether you are an experienced faculty member or new to the profession, you will invariably find surprises while conducting such evaluations. New faculty members will be astonished at the quality of some observations students make. I recall an acquaintance whose associates and he thought he had an effective sense of humor. However, after conducting a classroom evaluation, he was surprised to find that the students not only rated him low, but many felt he did not possess a sense of humor. (Whether or not the results of student sampling of this type precipitate a change in behavior of the faculty member is not important.) It is important, however, that faculty know how they are being perceived by the students.

There are two identifiable characteristics that are consistently valued by the students in relation to faculty behavior:

1.   Demonstrating business-like behavior in the classroom

2.   Being understanding and friendly

Figure 5 is a form that faculty members may use to conduct self-evaluation. Note that the form exists in three sections:

*   Classroom factors
*   Course-related factors
*   Personal evaluation factors

This form may be reproduced in its entirety; however, you may wish to add items, especially in sections two and three of the evaluation form.

The first section of the form (classroom evaluation) provides insight to classroom behavior as viewed by the students. The second section of the evaluation form (course related factors) may vary considerably depending upon the type of course. Some courses lend themselves extensively to course related factors while other classes may not. The final section (personal factors) gives faculty members an opportunity to select personal characteristics that they may wish to review occasionally. Questions may be added or deleted to this form at will.

Remember that student perceptions are very often motivated by personal biases rather than objective evaluation of the instructor, however, continued use of such a form helps faculty determine if there are characteristics that continue to surface that need attention. Many statistical techniques can be applied to evaluation forms such as this. A simple method of utilizing this form is to ask the students to assign numbers 1-5 to each of the categories and then weight them on a number scale. It is not intended that this self-evaluation form have content validity; however, it does give faculty members insight into their teaching.

Figure 5

## Faculty Evaluation Form

Class:_____

Date:_____

*Instructions: Please grade each factor on a scale of 1-5 in terms of your perception of the teacher's behavior or characteristics. (1=low; 5=high; NA for not applicable)*

### Classroom Factors

Preparation for class                                                    _____

Communication of classroom expectation to students       _____

Command of subject matter                                          _____

Course objectives were clearly defined                          _____

Course clearly reflected catalog description                   _____

Professional and business like classroom behavior         _____

Instructor preparation and organization                         _____

Tests and evaluation reflect classroom lecture,
    discussion and objectives                                        _____

Availability for consultation                                          _____

Encouragement of student participation                         _____

Instructor willingness to give individual help                 _____

Assignments clear and concise                                      _____

### Course Related Factors

Appropriateness of project assignments                        _____

Value of field trips                                                       _____

Appropriate topic selection for outside assignments       _____

Utilization of supplemental teaching aids,  support
    and other activities                                                _____

### Teacher Personal Evaluation

Consideration for differing opinions                              _____

Consideration for individuals as persons                        _____

Sense of humor                                                            _____

Overall rating of instructor                                           _____

Personal appearance                                                     _____

Consideration of students from different cultures            _____

Instructor's greatest strengths _____

Instructor's greatest weaknesses _____

Suggestions to improve course _____

# Teaching Techniques, Instructional Aids, and Testing

Chapter 3 is a discussion of some of the more common techniques, teaching aids and evaluation procedures utilized in modern classrooms. The techniques described herein, although not necessarily new or creative, have proven valuable over the years by successful instructors. It is the intent of this chapter to provide a variety of options for instruction, thus enabling instructors to incorporate a variety of classroom learning experiences.

## Teaching Techniques

Successful teaching depends to a certain degree upon the initiative, creativity, and risk-taking ability of the instructor. Even instructors with these characteristics, however, must also have a variety of techniques and approaches to be a successful teacher. Some of the more common techniques used by successful teachers include:

| | |
|---|---|
| Lecture | Discussion |
| Question/answer | Collaborative learning |
| Videos | Films |
| Field trips | Trade journals |
| Visiting speakers | Current publications |
| Handouts | Role playing |
| Buzz groups | Student panels |
| Projects | Student reports |

| | |
|---|---|
| Term papers | Outside assignments |
| Chalkboard | Overhead projections |
| Computer projections | Publications |
| Lab assignments | Computers |
| Case studies | Research projects |

These are but some of the possible activities to stimulate classroom instruction. One might start this chapter by checking off those techniques that have been utilized. The following pages describe in more detail some of these activities for classroom utilization.

### The Lecture

Although the lecture has long been recognized as one of the more appropriate ways to convey information, there is often a fine line between "telling" students and "presenting" a lecture. Historically, the lecture was intended for highly motivated and informed listeners who were present to hear a specific topic discussed. It has been adapted in recent times to nearly all classroom situations. It requires refinement and extensive preparation to present a successful lecture. The modern lecture involves the integration of technology and other activities into the total presentation. A good classroom lecture includes: motivation, information, explanation and conclusion.

Steps in building a better lecture include:
1. Build the lecture around major topics and objectives.
2. Include activities: a guest speaker, video, discussion, etc.
3. Introduce the lecture by telling the students the purpose of the lecture.
4. Do not read—refer to notes.
5. Over-prepare. It will enhance your confidence.
6. Use gestures. Remember a palm up is positive and down is negative.
7. Encourage students to interrupt.
8. Assist students in taking notes. Provide outlines

and/or pause for note taking.

9. Document references verbally.
10. Prepare anecdotes and questions.
11. Don't depend upon memory, write it down.
12. Move around. Don't stand in one place or by the lectern.
13. Tell them what you are going to tell them; tell them; then tell them what you told them.
14. Refer to examples or other topics.
15. Tell them when you are starting, what your intentions are, and when you are changing topics.
16. Summarize.

**Lecture Techniques.** Studies have shown that students retain more of the material presented in the early part of the lecture and less in the latter phases. Thus, it is important that significant points are made early and then reinforced by **activity** later in the presentation. There are several methods to improve lectures. Adequate preparation with appropriate support of references, anecdotes, and handouts will enhance the effectiveness of the lecture. Depending upon memory for such support may prove ineffective. Therefore, references, etc., should be written as part of the lecture notes. Physical appearance is also important; business-like approach and dress will pay off. An unkempt appearance will negate hours of diligent preparation. Cue the class to the major points to be stressed in the presentation. Allow students time to take notes. Provide a complete summary with repetition and reinforcement of important points. As indicated earlier, it is important that vocabulary and definitions be explained. Avoid buzz words and jargon. Use the chalkboard and other visual techniques as necessary. A lecture does **not** mean that only the instructor talks. It is important that time be allowed during the lecture for student feedback, questions, and discussions.

Some problems with lectures as described by students in various studies include being unable to clearly hear the instructor, rambling or deviation from the topic, poor support (board, overheads, etc.), vocabulary or material at inappropriate levels, and lack of opportunity to participate.

## Question/Answer

Questioning is an important tool that may be used to stimulate classroom participation. Many experienced instructors make it an unwritten rule to call upon every student in the class sometime during each class period. Be consicous of "gender bias," call on males and females equally. Pace questions so that students have time to phrase their answer. There are several reasons why questions are a good technique for classroom discussion. They include:

1. Stimulating thought.
2. Arousing curiosity.
3. Stimulating interest.
4. Developing student confidence in expressing themselves.
5. Determining student progress in class.
6. Reinforcing previous points.
7. Evaluating the preparation of students.

There is hardly a disadvantage associated with questioning if good judgment is exercised. Appropriate timing is important, as well as the type of questions and the vocabulary used. For example, it would be unkind to continue to question students who are embarrassed and are having difficulty responding. Some students need to be "brought along" in the classroom.

Good questioning involves several strategies. (1) Use open-ended questions when possible. That is, do not use questions that can be given a yes/no answer. (2) Use questions that elicit a comment or additional queries from students, even to the point of saying to a student, "What do you think of that, Kim?" (3) Questions should be part of the lesson plan. Prepare them ahead of time—don't wait for them to "happen."

Different types of questions have different purposes. They are usually found in three categories: content, discussion and stimulation. For example, a content question might be "What are the functions of a spreadsheet?" A discussion question might be "What are the advantages and disadvantages of a spreadsheet?" A stimulation question might be "How can spreadsheets enhance your job accuracy or a promotion?" This may be followed with

"What do you think of that?" One would not normally pose questions as testing. This often intimidates students and negates the purpose of the question/answer process. Questions should be addressed to individuals when possible, preferably by name, rather than to the whole class. If your class is giving you the silent treatment, question/answer can bail you out.

## The Demonstration

For classes that lend themselves to this technique, the demonstration is an effective way to teach skills because it involves two primary senses—seeing and hearing. Psychological researchers claim that nearly 90% of learning takes place with the involvement of these two senses. Demonstration has other advantages:

1. It is motivational.
2. It is an effective technique for varying activities in the classroom.
3. It attracts attention and can be presented to groups or to individual students.
4. It is effective for large group instruction.

The demonstration is probably under-utilized as a teaching tool. To be successful, demonstration requires extensive preparation. Although demonstration carries the risk that it will not be successful, this is a small risk as compared to the benefits gained if successful. Students normally will not be critical of teachers who are not successful while attempting to utilize complicated techniques. They are much more critical of boring repetitious classes. To adequately prepare, the instructor should simulate the demonstration prior to class presentation. This allows the teacher to examine the problems, be alert to possible difficulties, and even to forewarn the students that some steps are particularly difficult. Through this simple warning, the students will support the instructor and assist in making the demonstration successful.

Some guidelines for a successful demonstration include:

1. Double-check for enough and appropriate materials and tools. (The most common flaw in classroom demonstrations is "something is missing.")

    2. Complete checklist for materials and procedures.
       (Students can then "check" to assure correct procedure.)
    3. State and distribute the objectives of the demonstration.

## The Panel

The panel is an effective activity to stimulate student involvement. However, it must be structured in such a way that specific objectives and assignments are defined prior to the presentation of the panel. Normally, a panel should consist of two to four members. Each member of the panel should be assigned specific topics or issues to be presented and/or defended. After the presentation, discussion groups should be formed for the students to define their position concerning the topic. Helping students to develop open-ended questions to present to the rest of the class is an effective tool. A carefully structured panel is a valuable learning experience for the participants as well as the class.

## The Project

The project is an effective activity that will provide students the opportunity and experience of learning outside the classroom. Projects may consist of in-depth research into a class topic or a community based activity such as agency visitations, interviews, or case studies. A properly developed project will give students a variety of related activities from which to choose within their own sphere of interest. *After topics are selected, expectations of the students for completion of the project should be clarified. The project should weigh significantly in the final evaluation and assignment of a grade.*

## The Guest Lecturer

The guest lecturer is an under-utilized activity in most colleges. Most communities are rich with individuals who are willing, usually at no fee, to share their experience and expertise. The rapidly changing world in which we live makes it nearly impossible for faculty members to remain current on all issues. Inviting individuals who are on the cutting edge of changes in business, industry and community agencies is a very stimulating and informative activity for students. Again, it is necessary to structure such a visitation so that students are aware of the objectives of the activity. *Beware of the danger that students will interpret this activity as a guest speaker and become a listening audience rather than a participant.*

## The Case Study

The case study traditionally has been utilized mainly in sociology or psychology classes. The case study may, however, be used in many disciplines. Students may be given case studies of individuals or processes in finance, investing, historic contrast, geology and many other class situations. In a good case study, the instructor should establish the scenario, the objectives of the case, and the problem(s) that may be encountered. Students may then be given time to read and research the project and write their case paper or make an oral presentation. This may lead to student discussion in order to reach consensus or conclusion. Case studies are normally assigned to individual students and not to groups.

## Buzz Groups

The buzz group is an in-class activity. The purpose is to address a specific problem and do a comparison and contrast. The instructor identifies the discussion topic or problem and allows students to form small groups, usually three to five students. The students are given the freedom to develop their discussion guidelines in formulating a solution to the issue. The solution is formulated for presentation, possibly on a flip chart or overhead transparency for the following class session. Occasionally the instructor may have a solution prepared and use it as a discussion of the differences between the student buzz groups and the instructor's conclusions. Buzz groups should not be confused with small group projects. Buzz groups are employed as a short-term, quick conclusion 10 to 15 minute class activity.

## Field Trips

Field trips should be planned so that the entire session of the field trip is on location. The activities that the class will focus upon should be outlined prior to the trip. Arrange the class in small groups, specify to the students what they are to observe, and at the conclusion of the visit, meet to discuss the major points observed. The most effective field trips include credit toward the grade and require a written or oral report.

## Outside Readings/Written Assignments

Outside readings and additional assignments can be enhanced by the part-time instructor in several ways. Since neither the instructor nor the student is on campus for extensive library use, outside reading and references should be named in the syllabus. It will aid part-time students significantly if materials and periodicals are selected that are available in public libraries. The preparation of handouts with reference numbers also will assist students. This allows students to spend their time in the library actually using the materials rather than searching for them. Again, being specific in terms of the topic and objectives (and points counted toward the grade) are necessary for a successful outside assignment.

## Discussion/Critical Thinking

Good classroom discussion promotes independent thinking, motivates students, and stimulates creativity. It increases communication and helps students become active in the learning process. Discussion may be stimulated by utilizing critical thinking questions such as: "What is wrong with that kind of thinking?"; How else might that have been done?"; and "What are the strengths and weaknesses of this process?" Make certain that appropriate time is allowed for discussion to emerge. A good discussion uses positive reinforcement for students who participate. In a good discussion, students address each other, not the instructor. Most of all, know when to conclude and summarize the discussion. This may be accomplished with a warning, question, or request for a summary.

## Small Group/Large Group Instruction

Although not a specific classroom technique, there are different processes used in small group versus large group instruction.

Normally there are advantages to small group instruction because the informal atmosphere is an asset to both the instructor and the students. In small group, students have time to explore ideas without requiring a definite yes/no response, and both instructor and students have time for spontaneous feedback concerning established goals. Small groups, however, can have the weakness of too much incidental conversation which can make it difficult to have meaningful instruction. In addition, some students are more comfortable having the material presented to them in a structured format, and thus may be uncomfortable participating in a situation where they seem to be the center of discussion. It is necessary to encourage those students slowly in success activities at the beginning of the course.

Large classes are more impersonal and usually more difficult to teach. Successful large classes require greater preparation of materials, more handouts, and visuals. The importance of a good, well prepared lecture takes on added importance in large group instruction. If possible, arranging a 20 minute discussion group before and/or after class is helpful in helping students who are having trouble in a large group setting.

Some suggestions for easing the burden of teaching large classes include: (1) start positive—although a large group, the class is important and you are glad to be there; (2) identify clearly major points and questions; (3) use techniques such as buzz groups, panels, collaborative learning-don't assume that standard strategies don't work; (4) involve students in responses such as a show of hands or holding up colored cards (green for "I understand", red for "I don't understand"); (5) have students write a brief response paragraph to major questions and hand in; (6) keep a seating chart; (7) invite students for coffee in the cafeteria; and (8) move around—up the aisles, around the room as you lecture.

## Quality Control Circles

Quality circles is one of the most dynamic and interesting concepts that has evolved in the past decade. It is a management technique generally credited to the Japanese (Weimer, 1990). This technique can be very effective for instructors of adult students. It requires the involvement of employees (students) in some decision making activities of the class; is especially helpful for part-time teachers who do not have day contact with students; and is a relatively simple process.

During the first class session, the faculty member requests 5 or 6 volunteers to join the quality circle. The group meets periodically with the instructor, possibly during the coffee break or after class, to provide feedback concerning the progress of the class. The feedback might include comments concerning: lecture, discussion, homework, testing, or other class activities. This process provides an ongoing feedback mechanism that includes the involvement of students. It may also provide support as the instructor implements the circle's suggestions during the class presentation.

# Instructional Aids

Modern technological advances have made it possible for faculty to incorporate instructional aids in nearly any classroom situation. Gone are the days when one wheeled a large film projector into the room, made special arrangements for a screen, and called a projectionist to thread the film in order to show a simple 5-8 minute film. Although planning still requires scheduling, ordering, and the usual activities, it is far less complex than in the past. This section presents a brief description of some of the more commonly used teaching aids.

## Overhead Transparencies

The overhead projector has become one of the most popular support tools in education. It is unique in that it allows instructors to face the class while showing images on the screen using normal room lighting. Overhead projectors are inexpensive and are usually readily available. Overhead transparencies of notebook size can be easily prepared and retained and are practically indestructible. Some projectors are equipped with a roll that provides a continuous writing surface. This enables the retention of information on the roll in the event students later wish to discuss specific points. This is especially useful in mathematics, engineering, etc.

Overhead transparencies can be prepared by hand at very little cost and printed on most modern copiers. They may also be prepared professionally to provide multi-color or other desired features. Use at least 24 point letters.

Overhead transparencies have several advantages over other types of media aids.

1. The equipment is easy to procure, often available without reservation or check-out.

2. The equipment is easy to use, usually requiring simply that it be plugged into a wall socket and focused. Sometimes the most difficult operation on an overhead projector is finding the on/off switch. In modern overheads, it is usually a bar across the front or hidden along the side to the rear of the base.

3. Overhead transparencies are stimulating for the class because they utilize both audio and visual activities.

4. There is no limit to the artistic excellence that can be produced on a transparency. Many faculty members easily prepare their own transparencies. Transparencies may be typewritten, handwritten, or drawn on standard size plain white paper, and instantaneously produced on a standard copier. Many times it is worth the extra effort to make a professional looking overhead transparency. They are easily maintained, durable, and thus can be a permanent part of future presentations.

5. The use of overhead transparencies adds a professional touch to teaching situations.

6. They can be used in normal classroom conditions. No special lighting is needed, and if a screen is not available, they can be shown on a wall.

Faculty members who have not utilized overhead transparencies in their classroom presentations should write themselves an objective to develop some for their next teaching assignment. It is one of the few instructional aids that seems to have several advantages and few notable disadvantages.

## Video Tape

Probably the most effective modern instructional aid is the video tape. With the reduction in cost of camcorders and tape itself, the possibilities for expanded use are nearly endless. Most institutions now have equipment for instructors who wish to develop their own scenario as well as a library of tapes that may be applicable to your class. Videos are not only attention getters, but provide the opportunity for direct student involvement. Some instructors even allow students to tape themselves for oral reports and submit the tape for evaluation. Video provides an attractive option for part-time students as well as part-time instructors. Video tapes provide all the advantages of movie film without the disadvantages.

## Using Multimedia

**Multimedia in the Classroom.** Exciting developments in computing technology are becoming available to the classroom teacher. Colleges are beginning to provide multimedia laboratories for the development of instructional materials, support staff to consult with faculty, and multimedia computer equipment for the classroom. These facilities allow faculty to include a wide variety of media directly into their classroom presentations.

Multimedia presentation software programs allow teachers to seamlessly integrate text, audio, animation, high resolution graphical images, and full-motion video in classroom presentations. This form of instructional aid is limited only by the creativity of the instructor and the equipment available at the college. The ability to include different media elements into the classroom increase the potential for learning.

Multimedia software is increasingly included with standard textbook materials from publishers. These materials on floppy disks, CD-ROMs (Compact Disc Read Only-Memory), and/or laserdiscs include interactive text, audio, animation, still images and full motion video. Compatible electronic equipment needs to be available in the classroom in order for the teacher to utilize these materials.

College computing services or media services departments often provide support for standard software across the campus. Contact the appropriate department on your campus to see what equipment, software and support services are provided to assist teaching faculty in the development of their classroom materials.

**Electronic Communications.** The "information age" is making an impact on educational institutions around the world. Adjunct/Part-Time faculty may be able to access the campus electronic network and the vast resources of Internet. Electronic mail can foster communications between students and the teacher who may not regularly be on campus. Connection to the Internet can provide many resources that supplement materials introduced in the classroom. These tools provide the teacher with increased flexibility as a *facilitator of learning* (See section on Teaching Strategies-Chapter 4).

*"Using Multimedia" contributed by Richard G. Clemens, Ed. D., Director of Instructional Technology/Multimedia Laboratory, Wright State University, Dayton, OH.*

## Flipchart

A commonly used instructional aid for business seminars is a simple flipchart. When adapted to the classroom, the flipchart has many advantages over the chalkboard or overhead projector. The flipchart, a large tablet with pages that can be turned vertically, is especially useful for allowing students in small groups to record their discussions and their conclusions. It is also utilized by the instructor for recording major points of a presentation to which descriptive lists may be added. The information can then be retained by tearing off the page and taping it to the wall for future reference. A flipchart and felt tip pen can be very effective tools in adding to the active classroom.

## Handouts

Although somewhat overused in the past, handouts are still a valuable instrument for instructors. Modern copy technology and computer printers allow for ease of preparation and update. Handouts should be used for material that students will need for reference, such as important definitions and computations, or position statements to be discussed and contrasted. Handouts for lecture purposes should contain only an outline of the material discussed with space for students to add their own comments. A serious note of caution: *be careful of copyright violations!*

# Tests and Testing

Faculty must make every effort to prepare students for the their evaluation in the course. This process starts by informing students at the beginning of the class of the testing procedure; when tests will be given, and the criteria upon which they will be based. Too often students are heard to criticize instructors with the statement, "They didn't test over what they talked about in class."

It should also be remembered that testing is not only used for evaluation of the students, it also provides the instructor with valuable information concerning their success in reaching the objectives of the course. The major types of tests used in college classes are: multiple choice, essay, and recall. In special circumstances, performance, oral, and short answer tests may also be utilized.

**Essay Tests.** Essay tests are very popular for college courses. They are effective at any level of the learning hierarchy. Although essay tests require considerable time for students to respond, they give an in-depth perspective in terms of overall student achievement.

There are several factors to remember when writing test questions that require essay answers. Most important is the fact that essay questions should reflect the **objectives written for the course.** They should incorporate a significant amount of content, including discussion, contrasting, comparing etc. Short answer questions are too easily answered with an unexplained yes/ no. Finally, be certain that the student has the background to respond adequately in terms of vocabulary, content, and subject covered, and that questions are clear without chance of ambiguity.

Grading of essay questions presents the greatest difficulty. Keep in mind that essay questions are asking students to be objective, yet justify. The appropriate way to grade an essay response is to list important items for the response and prioritize them, assigning more points to the highest priorities. Be aware of questions that only solicit students' opinions. It is impossible to assign evaluation points to opinions.

**Multiple Choice Tests.** Multiple choice tests are probably the most popular tests used today. With the advent of computer scoring, they not only are efficient in terms of time consumed, but they are easy, through item analysis techniques, to determine the most valid questions. Still there is considerable skill involved in constructing multiple choice questions. Some suggestions for constructing good multiple choice questions are:

1. Provide four possible responses to minimize the guess factor.
2. Do not include impossible responses.
3. Do not use "none of the above" or "all of the above."
4. Be consistent with the format so students are not confused with wording or punctuation changes.
5. Do not use qualifiers such as "always" or general qualifiers such as "usually."
6. State questions in a positive format.
7. Keep choices approximately the same length.

Some disadvantages of multiple choice tests are: they often test at only the knowledge level rather than analysis and synthesis; they provide opportunity for guessing; and they depend primarily on recall and memory.

**Recall and Completion Tests.** Recall items may be posed as simple questions, completion, or brief response. Used too often, these tests tend to encourage students to memorize rather than understand. There are, however, advantages to recall tests. They are relatively simple to grade and construct; they can address a broad field of content; and they require specific recall rather than guessing or rationalization.

Some suggestions for developing recall questions are:

1. Give information concerning the answer prior to the answer blank.

2. Qualify information so students are clear concerning the response and cannot generalize.
3. Try to include responses at the analysis and synthesis level.
4. Pose questions so that only one correct response is possible.
5. Allow sufficient and *equal* space for the response.

**True/False Tests.** Although true/false tests are not held in high regard at the college level, there may be occasion when, for a specific purpose, they may be utilized. For example, when a large amount of material is to be tested quickly or students need a stimulating activity. Some points to remember in constructing true/false questions include:

1. Avoid ambiguous words.
2. Avoid patterns of responses such as a string of true's.
3. Avoid direct quotes.
4. Avoid specific descriptors or adjectives.

# Grading

## The Basics

Grading of students is probably the most difficult task for faculty. All of the elements of teaching, preparation, presentation, and student activity, are reflected in the grading process. In addition, in an era of accountability, teachers are sometimes called upon to justify grades with documentation. Thus, establishment of firm criteria for grading is necessary. There are some general rules that are helpful in establishing the grading process. They are listed below:

1. Communicate grading criteria clearly to the students.
2. Include criteria other than test scores.
3. Avoid irrelevant factors such as tardiness.
4. Weigh grading criteria carefully—have a plan.
5. Grade students on their achievement, not other students'.

## Evaluation Plan

In order to clearly define and delineate the criteria for assignment of grades, it is necessary to develop a grading plan. An evaluation plan is a simple device in chart or work sheet form. The plan contains all of the factors that apply to the evaluation of the students and the assignment of a grade. The factors are identified and listed with assigned weight to each factor. The following chart is an example of a grading plan.

## Evaluation Chart

| Grade Factors | Percent of Final Grade | Possible Points | Points Received |
|---|---|---|---|
| Tests | 60 | 90 | _____ |
| Paper | 20 | 30 | _____ |
| Project | 10 | 15 | _____ |
| Class Participation | 10 | 15 | _____ |
| Totals | 100 | 150 | _____ |

Note that this type of plan allows the freedom to assign any number of criteria or points to any activity because the percentage will always come out to 100%.

# Teaching Adult Students

Although it is difficult to adequately plan in a standard way for all classes, there are fundamental activities that can be utilized for teaching adult students. Keeping in mind that even these activities must be constantly reassessed to meet changing institutional and cultural needs, this chapter is intended to provide a better understanding of today's students so that an appropriate assessment of classroom skills can be made.

## Student Characteristics

Today's students, whether they are older adults or college age, possess some common traits that affect classroom attitudes. These attitudes are based upon the concept that students may view themselves as consumers of a product, rather than seekers of knowledge. As indicated earlier, they will expect well-planned and prepared course goals and objectives. Other characteristics to be recognized include:

* Today's students are more self-directed than their earlier counterparts. In other words, they generally know what they want and where they are going.

* Today's students are highly demanding as consumers. They feel that they are paying for their education and are entitled to a product. There have been legal cases in which colleges have been required to provide evidence of delivering advertised services (classes).

* Today's students often come to the classroom with rich life and educational experiences. They have read broadly and often have had interesting employment and travel experiences they may wish to share.

* Today's students expect to be treated as adults. They want to be treated on an equal basis and not as students or "kids".

* Today's students will demand relevance and immediate application of their learning. Relevance today, unlike the 60's, is relevance toward achieving a goal or a career rather than social change.

*Although the students are more demanding, they are also more interesting, more challenging, and will contribute to a happy, optimistic learning experience if given the opportunity.* Most adult students are not in the classroom to compete. They are there to succeed and improve themselves. Teachers of adults should minimize the concept of competition and increase the concept of class cooperation and success. Above all, the age old process of "x" number of A's, "x" number of B's, etc. based upon the normal curve, has been abandoned in the modern classroom.

## Student Learning Styles

Student learning styles are based upon the theory that there are differing methods for gathering, organizing, and evaluating information. Some people have consistent ways of selecting information and have dominant styles while others are more flexible in their approaches. Some people prefer to learn a skill by manipulating concrete objects, some by listening, some by reading a manual, and some by interacting with others. In brief, people have unique and characteristic ways of using their mind (Kazmierski, 1977).

Another expert on learning styles outlines a more structured system called the "4mat system". This system identifies four specific traits of learners. They are: the imaginative learners, the analytic learners, the common sense learners, and the dynamic learners.

**Imaginative learners** will expect the faculty member to produce authentic curricula, knowledge upon which to build, involvement in group work, and will provide feedback. They care about fellow students and the instructor.

**Analytic learners** are more interested in theory and what the experts think, need details and data, and are uncomfortable with subjectiveness. They expect the class to enhance their knowledge and place factual knowledge over creativity.

**Common sense** learners test theories and apply common sense, are problem solvers, and are skill oriented. They expect to be taught skills and may not be flexible or good in teamwork situations.

**Dynamic learners** believe in self discovery. They like change and flexibility, are risk takers, and are at ease with people. They may, however, be pushy and manipulative. They respond to dynamic instructors who are constantly trying new things (McCarthy, 1987).

It is important to understand that these differing types of learners may be present in any given class. This makes it necessary for the instructor to possess the ability to use a variety of classroom activities.

I recall an experience while teaching as a college adjunct faculty member that relates to this topic. Having for years been successful teaching classes by encouraging open communication and maximizing student involvement, I experienced a class in which an acquaintance was enrolled. This person simply would not respond or take part in discussions. Knowing this person to be social and bright, I was not completely surprised that when all the criteria for grades were considered, the individual easily earned an "A", contrary to my belief that all students must participate to learn! It was only later that I realized that the student process for learning was not flawed, it was just different from the style that I, as the instructor, had perceived necessary for learning.

It is important that you review closely the previous paragraphs because within the description of the student types is an important factor. That is, just as students have learning styles, teachers have teaching styles. Thus, you might identify your own teaching style from the above description. It is important that you understand your teaching style and behaviors and modify or understand that style in order to accommodate all learners.

# Motivation

Students are motivated for many reasons: individual improvement, intellectual curiosity, needed employment competencies, change of or advancing career, employment requirement, or the completion of degree or certificate requirements. Although these motivational reasons are broad and varied, faculty must possess the skills to motivate students with a variety of approaches including occasional risk taking.

The following anecdote exemplifies such risk taking. After many years of teaching, I remember being faced with a class that would not respond or participate. Admittedly it was a Friday night class; however, you might expect that in such a class, highly motivated students would be enrolled. They were, however, very tired students and many of them were enrolled merely to pick up additional credits. After teaching the class about three weeks and experiencing very little student response, on the spur of the moment during the third evening, I simply stated, "We must start communicating. I would like each of you at this time to turn to a person near you, introduce yourself and tell them that you are going to help them get through the course, no matter how difficult it is, that you will be there to help them whenever they become confused, and that the two of you (by helping each other) can be successful in this course." This seemingly simple technique worked wonders. The students became acquainted with someone they hadn't known previously, and in many cases, found someone who really **could** help them get through the course. For the remainder of the course, when it appeared that the class was experiencing difficulty, I simply needed to say "lets take a few minutes and get together with our partner." When chalkboard work was given, two students would voluntarily go to the board together. Thus a previously unused "risk" activity proved successful—and was my first experience with collaborative learning and the partner system. This is an example of trying a basic technique of motivation. In this case it worked. It may not work every time, but it was not a technique that I had in my repertoire prior to that time. So, in introducing this topic, motivation of adult students, be reminded that faculty must occasionally try motivational techniques that are not found in the literature; however there are proven techniques that should be in the professional portfolio of all teachers.

## Maslow's Hierarchy

It is virtually impossible to incorporate all theories of motivation for your students. It is appropriate, therefore, that we find refuge in a time honored theory of learning called ***Maslow's Hierarchy of Needs***. Maslow's hierarchy states that the basic needs of human beings fall into five categories: physiological, safety, love and belonging, esteem, and self-actualization:

1. PHYSIOLOGICAL—*feeling good physically with appropriate food and shelter.*
2. SAFETY—*the feeling of security in one's environment.*
3. LOVE AND BELONGING OR THE SOCIAL NEED—*fulfilling the basic family and social role.*
4. ESTEEM—*the status and respect of a positive self-image.*
5. SELF-ACTUALIZATION—*growth of the individual.*

**Physiological, Safety, Love and Belonging.** The fact that Maslow's needs are in hierarchy form is a major problem for teachers of adults. Attempting to address the needs of esteem and self-actualization in the classroom, when physiological, safety, and love and belonging needs have not been met, is a monumental task. In fact, the lack of fulfillment of the basic needs may interfere with the learning process. This interference may manifest itself in anti-social behavior. The characteristics of the negative classroom are discussed in the section on ***Student Behavior p.58.***

The challenge becomes, how does one in a short period of time, teaching on a part-time basis to mostly part-time students, overcome all of these barriers? The fact is that one may not overcome all of these barriers. If instructors attempt to take the time to analyze each of the unmet needs of each of their students, they will have little time to work toward the goals and objectives of the course. There is, however, an important factor to support the instructor. It is that the need to achieve appears to be a basic need in human beings. The need to achieve, an intrinsic motivator that usually overcomes most of the other distractions to learning, is the factor upon which successful teachers capitalize. There is little that faculty can do to help students to meet the physiological, safety, and love and belonging needs. The need for *esteem* and *self-actualization,* which are essentially achievement, are areas in which teaching strategies can be implemented.

**Esteem.** Esteem is the status and respect with which human beings are regarded by their peers. Faculty members can incorporate activities that assist students in achieving status and self-respect, supporting fulfillment of the esteem need. This is accomplished by providing an environment in which students can experience success in their learning endeavors. *Many learning theorists claim that success in itself is the solution to motivation and learning.* One of the great fallacies in teaching is often stated by students who have succeeded in classes where other students have dropped out. That observation is: "That prof was tough, but he/she was really good." This may or may not be true. *The fact is that being tough has absolutely no relationship to being good.* Too often the reverse of this statement is generalized and some faculty emphasize toughness as a substitute for good teaching. There is no evidence to suggest that "tough teachers" are better teachers than those who are "not so tough." It is especially discouraging to marginal students who are working hard when the chances for success experiences are negated by the instructor's desire to be tough.

Building esteem through success experiences is accomplished in many ways. Following are some suggestions that can be incorporated into classroom instruction to assist students to experience success.

*1. Make certain that students are aware of course requirements.* Students should be provided with course objectives in written form that tell them what they are expected to accomplish.

*2. Inform students precisely what is expected of them.* This means not only the work or the knowledge necessary for them to complete the course content, but also the time commitment.

*3. Give students non-verbal encouragement whenever possible.* There are many ways this can be accomplished. Eye contact with students can very often elicit a positive response. Gestures are important. The hand pointing upward is positive, downward is negative. A smile, a nod of the head, just looking at students with the feeling that they are working in a pleasant environment is in itself effective non-verbal encouragement.

*4. Give positive reinforcement at every opportunity.* Simple techniques such as quizzes for which grades are not taken, quizzes designed so most or all students will succeed, as well as short tests as a supplement to grading are effective positive reinforcement strategies. Comments written on hand-in papers, tests, and projects are effective ways to provide positive feedback. Of course, the ideal form of positive reinforcement is provided through individual conferences and informal conversations with students at chance meetings.

*5. Provide a structured situation in which the students feel comfortable.* The laissez-faire classroom is generally a lazy classroom. It is generally agreed that the structured setting with students participating in activities is much better than an unstructured approach.

*6. Provide opportunity for discussion of outside experiences by students.* Some students in your class, who may not be particularly adept at the course content, may have significant contributions and accomplishments to share. One of the greatest builders of esteem is to allow students to share their success experiences with others.

**Self-Actualization.** Self-actualization is the realization of individual growth. Such growth is realized through achievement and success. Self-actualization is the highest of Maslow's hierarchy. Course planning for enhancement of student self-actualization is the ultimate in successful teaching. The suggestions listed here can assist in the student growth process.

*1. Each class should offer a challenge to each student.* Challenges are presented in a variety of ways. If they are insurmountable challenges they become barriers, therefore, it is important that faculty plan activities appropriate for the course. Grades are challenges; however, grades must be achievable or they cause frustration. Achieving class credit is a challenge. Most students, even though they may not achieve the grade desired, will feel satisfied if they obtain the credit for which they are working.

Assigning incompletes and allowing additional time for projects are techniques utilized to assist students in obtaining credit for their work. Questions, if properly phrased, can become challenges.

*2. Problem Solving.* The ultimate challenge in the classroom is problem solving. Problem solving techniques vary greatly depending upon the subject matter. Although it is impossible to discuss in detail here the ramifications of problem solving, this challenge does not lend itself solely to scientific and mathematics classes. It can also be utilized in many other courses through discussion, professional journals, literature, outside projects, case studies and group work.

*3. Treat students as individuals.* Individual conferences and the development of a system to allow students to get to know their instructors and other students are important. Many experienced faculty members do not hesitate to share with students their home or business phone number. Usually they are quite surprised at how seldom it is used.

*4. Be cautious not to prejudge students.* Unfortunately, stereotyping still exists in classrooms today. Faculty must make every effort not to "type" classes or students as "good" or "bad." Such stereotyping will affect grading and attitudes toward the students. Also, there is a good chance that the judgment may be incorrect. *There is no place for stereotypes in education.*

*5. Treat students as adults.* Many of today's students hold powerful positions in business and industry. It is difficult for them to regard the teacher as someone superior. To adult students the instructor is just someone in a different role. Above all don't refer to them as "kids."

*6. Give consideration to student's personal problems when possible.* Giving adult students personal consideration implies that rules concerning attendance, paper deadlines, tardiness, etc., may be flexible when faced with the realities of the lives of adult students. Practice flexibility whenever possible.

# Classroom Strategies for Teaching Adults

## Teacher Behaviors

Being prepared with tried and proven strategies to assist student learning is important. Some principles to remember are:

*1. The teacher is a facilitator of learning.* Students do not expect teachers to know all there is to know about the subject—they do expect, however, the teacher to facilitate their learning the facts and skills of the course.

*2. Understand your teaching situation.* As an adjunct faculty member you may have a variety of assignments in differing institutions. When making your preparation consider the following questions: Is this class part of a competitive program? Are the goals clarified for the student and the institution? Can student projects be developed to meet the student's needs?

*3. Allow for individual differences.* The diversity of adult learners today is significant. Allow for this by giving individual help, knowing student's names, and being aware of differing backgrounds.

*4. Vary teaching activities.* Use different activities in the classroom. Try new ideas. Some experts recommend changing activities every 20 minutes.

*5. Develop a supportive climate.* Students must be made to feel that you are there to support them in the learning process, not prove how tough the course is.

*6. Be sensitive to barriers.* Some baggage students bring with them include: unsuccessful previous educational experience, the time barrier, confusion concerning college (procedures) in general, failure to understand their academic limitations, stress, physical and mental handicaps.

Although there are not prescribed procedures to address all of the above, you should prepare yourself to be effective in all of these roles. Professional reading, discussions with colleagues and mentors, and teaching workshops will assist you in the development of necessary skills. The overriding strategy that applies is "be understanding and considerate."

## Student Behaviors

During your teaching tenure you will experience differing classroom behavior from students that challenges your ability to maintain the class in a constructive and positive manner. Some of the more common challenges and suggestions for remedies follows. Keep in mind that the suggestions are simply observations of other teachers and may not apply to all situations.

**The Class Expert.** This person has all or most of the answers and is more than willing to share them—and argue if he or she is not right. Suggestion: Allow other students to react, give respondent time to tell anecdotes and/or present position, remind "expert" and the class that they must get back to the objectives of the course.

**The Quiet Class.** Use questioning techniques, group work, partner system, current events, personal experiences, brainstorming, icebreakers.

**The Talkative Class.** Allow time for conversation, specify time for class work to begin, exert your control.

**The Negative Student.** Initially ignore, invite to a conference, provide success experience, determine interest of student and cultivate it.

**The Off-the-subject Student.** Allow some freedom for discussion and reaction of other students—other students will usually provide incentive to get back on the subject—seize the opportunity and stress the need to get back to course objectives.

**The Unruly Student.** Try all of the above; if situation becomes serious you have the welfare of all students at stake—dismiss class and seek help.

## Critical Thinking

Critical thinking can best be stimulated by raising questions and by offering challenges about a specific issue or statement. Many students still like the "right" answer from the instructor. Critical thinking in instruction goes far beyond that. Critical thinking involves asking the right kind of questions and goes so far as letting students develop assumptions and analyze (either in groups or individually) those assumptions. They may then examine alternatives to their assumptions.

Some types of questions to ask might be: "What is the source of your information and how reliable is it?" "What are your personal experiences in relation to the information?" "What are differing positions?" "What are your feelings on the topic?" "Why?" "Do you agree?" Allow think and wait time. If students take a position on an issue, ask them for an alternate position.

## Cooperative (Collaborative) Learning

Cooperative learning (also called collaborative learning), one of the oldest educational techniques, is making a comeback in college classrooms. In theory, cooperative learning brings students with differing abilities together into small groups where they teach each other the concepts of the class by reinforcing lecture and text materials. In practice, students either work on specific projects cooperatively or take selected quizzes and/or tests together. The process forces all students to become actively involved in classroom activities. Adult learners relate to cooperation in the classroom because of the cooperation required in most workplaces.

For instructors, the two basic prerequisites of cooperative learning are thorough planning and a *total* commitment. As a facilitator the instructor becomes an idea person, a resource person, a mediator (conflict resolution is as much of an accomplishment in cooperative education as it is in the workplace or in life itself), and a supporter of the students' efforts. Virtually all academic and technical disciplines can benefit from this technique.

Preliminary planning includes a discussion of classroom goals, specific activities that can be assigned cooperatively, and the balance sought between traditional and cooperative classroom activities. If grades are going to be assigned for group work the students must be made aware of this at the beginning of the term; the assignment of the same grade to each member of a group is the incentive needed to make cooperative learning work effectively.

The optimum size for a work group is four or five students; more students can be unwieldy while fewer opens the door to domineering students. Groups can be formed by (1) students themselves, (2) the instructor assigning students to a group, (3) random assignment, or (4) selection based upon similar interests or specific criteria. Decided disadvantages of student-based selection are that students may choose to be with friends, which excludes assimilation of new students into the mainstream of the class, and there may be stress in arranging groups if students do not know each other and have no basis for selection.

The benefits of cooperative learning include: adults have a vehicle to get to know others in class; attendance tends to be better (a result of a commitment to the group); improved grades due to an increased understanding of the subject matter; classroom groups lead to study groups outside of class; and students become participants in their own learning.

Teachers regularly must re-evaluate their classroom styles to accommodate changes in technology, abilities of students, and demands of students. Cooperative learning is but one of many viable strategies to encourage participation by students. Obstacles that might be encountered are: some students feel they have paid money to take the course, therefore the teacher is expected to stand in front of the class and lecture; groups may not take an assignment seriously; and some individuals may have difficulty working within a group. However, problems can be overcome by involving students in decisions regarding cooperative activities.

Adults are sensitive to how others view them and tend to be more candid when working in small groups; working with fellow students provides adults the opportunity to explore new horizons in your subject area.

*"Cooperative Learning" contributed by Arlene Sego, author of Cooperative Learning-A Classroom Guide (see references).*

### Feedback

As has been indicated in other parts of this publication, obtaining student feedback is instrumental to good instruction. Most instructors rely upon student questions and responses in class for their feedback. Good feedback, however, is too important to leave to chance.

The faculty evaluation form at the end of Chapter 2 and the section on "Quality Circles" in this publication are examples of feedback. The institution in which you teach may have such prepared instruments that can be of value. All such instruments have weaknesses as well as strengths, whether they be open-ended or closed-end questions, rating forms or checklists. Given the time constraints facing most adjunct faculty, there are a few techniques that provide immediate and helpful feedback. They are:

1. Prior to testing, give the class sample test questions which are not counted toward the grade, and ask them to write responses to the questions as well as the content.

2. Maintain open and on-going verbal communication, especially concerning clarity of assignments and deadlines.

3. At the end of the course, have the students write a letter to "Aunt Millie" describing the course to her, then collect it.

4. Do not confuse feedback with evaluation. Feedback is an opportunity for you to relate to your students and to enhance your class.

Some additional methods for obtaining feedback are:

| | |
|---|---|
| class discussion | study guides |
| group discussions course | post-mortem |
| student conference | paper comments |
| quizzes | quality circles |

## Summary

The previous paragraphs have discussed activities and techniques for the building of esteem and self-actualization of students. If instructors spend just 20% of their time on techniques related to the behaviors described here, the rewards will be exciting.

It is the belief of many educators that motivation is basically intrinsic. It is inside the beholder. It may be stimulated by external forces but must be cultivated by the learner. Instructors cannot develop a set of procedures to guarantee motivation of all students. Faculty can, however, be a "significant other" in the motivational process. *The best way to motivate students is to be a motivated teacher.*

# Some Practical Teaching Suggestions—From Teachers

This chapter is a compilation of teaching tips, suggestions and experiences submitted by successful instructors. The chapter contains discipline specific suggestions as well as techniques and strategies of a general nature. The identification of the contributor is shown with each item. We are grateful to the writers for their contributions, making this chapter possible.

## Study Partners: Conquering Inaccessibility and Fear

As an adjunct/part-time English faculty member and often a teacher of adults, I face two unique obstacles:

1) Since I am not on campus everyday, students are sometimes frustrated by their inability to stop by my office anytime. For example, if my classes meet only on Tuesdays and Thursdays, and students miss a Thursday class, they may not see me until the following week to ask questions or make up work. Also, since many of my students work full time during the day and attend classes in the evening, I am sometimes frustrated by my inability to contact them, especially if they have missed several classes or assignments.

2) A second dilemma is overcoming the insecurity and doubts that many older students experience upon returning to school after an absence of many years. They often need extra encouragement and a boost of confidence. Fear of asking "stupid" questions or

embarrassing themselves can result in lack of progress or even failure.

To promote success, I have instituted the use of study partners in each of my classes. After a first day get-acquainted activity, I assign or allow students to choose a "study partner." This partner is responsible for:

1. Taking notes and assignments/handouts for the partner when he/she is absent.

2. Handing in or collecting a paper for the absent partner.

3. Answering/discussing the unasked questions, which students may think are too simple to ask.

4. Possibly studying for a quiz or proofreading a paper.

In my experience study partner interaction has provided several positive results. It promotes accountability for students and saves my time. For example, a student can no longer come to see me and say, "I don't have my assignment because I was not here on Tuesday and I didn't know about it." If students cannot contact me, it is their responsibility to contact their study partners. I no longer accept excuses for late papers or requests to make up quizzes or tests, and I rarely must re-teach a lesson to an absent student.

The best result of all is that students who actively participate with their study partners earn higher grades and feel much more confident about their abilities. Also, a positive atmosphere for learning and future work is established and encouraged.

Kathy M. Richards
PA College of Technology
Williamsport, PA

## Managing The Learning Environment

The adult learner is a very unique individual, with a very unique set of learning objectives and abilities. The teacher of adults, then, needs to be aware of these priority shifts, and determine processes which will optimize cooperative learning opportunities. In the end, the major role of the teacher of adults is to manage the learning environment (the adult learner is perfectly capable of managing her/himself).

This is at once immensely liberating and immensely challenging for the educator. The best hope is to develop strategies for managing the classroom. Following are some suggestions:

**Step One.   Develop Mutual Respect and Mutual Trust.**

Being effective in working and learning with others begins by having unconditional respect for every other human being. The first step in developing mutual respect is to offer it. This will go a long way toward developing mutual trust, and will help eliminate power struggles.

**Step Two.   Neutralize The Learning Environment.**

Your adult students and you will bring a lot of baggage into the classroom, baggage from family, work, school and personal life. No learning will take place until the baggage is checked. (Baggage of value can be reclaimed after class.)   You are not responsible for taking care of your students, but you are responsible for caring about them. Learning the difference is a milestone in learning. Whatever it takes, you must offer some process (no tricks) which will invite your co-learners to set aside their cares and concerns and engage in meaningful learning activity. Current events which tie into the course focus lend themselves well to this process.

**Step Three.   Know The Course Learning Objectives, Your Students, Learning Objectives, and Your Own, And Know How To Accomplish All Of These.**

Whatever you do in the classroom, it should have relevance to the learning objectives. The course learning objectives should already be in writing. If not, set them down and share them with your students. Know and be willing to declare your own. Work with full energy to accomplish these. Ask your students, professional colleagues and supervisors to evaluate your progress from time to time. Correct your processes whenever necessary.

**Step Four.   Keep A Learning Journal.**

Before the course begins, perform an initial self-assessment. Set down what you already know about teaching this subject, teaching this course, and teaching the adult learner. Keep a personal learning journal, especially documenting learning breakthroughs. Incorporate them into your next teaching experience.

**Step Five.   Remember Learning Is Fun.**

Anytime you are not excited to enter the classroom, anytime you don't get excited during class, and anytime you don't leave the classroom excited, take stock in what is going on. No one ever said adult education would be easy. It should, however, be enjoyable for both you and your students.

**Step Six.   Remember You Have What It Takes To Be Successful.**

A very wise man and a very great teacher once said, "To be

successful as a teacher requires three things only: you must love your subjects, love your students, and love to teach." He might have added, "All the rest you can learn."

Robert R. Dolan
City University
Renton, WA

# A Reading (Or Any Class) Ice-Breaker

An important part of teaching is self-esteem building, especially in basic skills classes such as I teach in reading at Ivy Tech, Elkhart. I have incorporated several exercises into my reading course which serve as self-esteem builders. One of these I introduce the first night of class as a kind of ice-breaker.

I give each student a questionnaire to fill out which helps me get to know each of them and helps them think about reading and what they want out of the reading class. But I also ask them to answer at the end of the questionnaire a question which is somewhat different. I ask them to share a little information about themselves that most people don't know. I stress that this is not to be very private information, but rather something unique or unusual.

To help them get on with the task, I give them examples such as the mother who reported having triplets or the student who got a personal call from a former president or another student who said he had 10,000 sports cards. Even after giving several examples, some students still look blank. So I give them more general suggestions such as describing pets, travel experiences, awards, wishes for the future, family history, etc. Next I explain what I intend to do with the information. I tell them that I'll hold it and give it back to them in several weeks. However, I explain that I'll do this by compiling their answers without their names. During the regular class break, they will then try to identify who wrote what.

I keep the information until a little class spirit has begun to develop, that is, until they have begun to feel more comfortable with each other. When I give them their lists, I instruct them to ask only "yes" or "no" questions, such as, "Do you . . . ?" or "Are you the one who . . . ?" (I also add a comment about myself to add interest to the exercise for everyone.)

Usually when the class comes back from break, the students are eager to review their lists together. The first time I did this exercise, one student came smiling to me after break and said, "You did it again!" When I looked a little startled, he said the game had created quite a buzz of activity in the lounge.

Reviewing answers in class usually generates more discussion about what each person had written about himself or herself. This discussion adds further to the spirit of the exercise.

A simple exercise such as this takes little effort to execute. But it is just one small way in which students can feel noticed and appreciated by the instructor and by each other.

Myrna Burkholder
Ivy Tech
Elkhart, IN

## Who Am I?

Most educators agree that collaborative activities foster cooperation, open up a world of ideas to the individual student, and prepare students to live and work successfully in the multicultural world they will surely inhabit.

Who Am I? is a multifaceted activity that generates a substantial amount of information, even on the first day of class.

(1) Who Am I? serves as a diagnostic giving me the opportunity to assess a student's writing ability before the class actually begins. If a student demonstrates serious deficiencies, I may recommend that he or she drop back a course level.

(2) Who Am I? provides each student the opportunity to write an essay-autobiography in which she or he selects life events that are significant to them as individuals.

(3) Who Am I? suggests that students begin to think of multiculturalism as a continuing series of life-enhancing encounters which they (in all likelihood) have already experienced, and not just a new term or method the teacher is imposing upon them for ten weeks.

(4) Who Am I? allows me to assess individual learning styles from the student's perspective. I have found that most students are very aware of who they are as individual learners; they know and can describe quite accurately the conditions under which they produce their best academic work.

(5) Who Am I? gives students a candid opportunity to tell me how they feel about course content, requirements, and the class itself. Simply having the opportunity to express concern—or confidence—suggests to students that I, their teacher, really do care about them as individuals, not merely as names in a grade book.

(6) Finally, Who Am I? encourages students to set personal goals that go beyond "getting an A," and to take personal responsibility for achieving those goals.

When students respond to Who Am I? they are making the first vital move toward success in the classroom—they are trusting me with their lives, hopes and dreams on paper. I respond to each student, in writing, by reacting (not evaluating or judging) to what they tell me. The admiration I have for each person's achievements and her or his courage in pursuing education, often against formidable odds, comes through clearly in my responses. In this way I am able to establish myself as a partner in our mutual learning encounter over the next ten weeks.

## WHO AM I?

Please write an essay which includes the following information. This is my way of getting to know you as an individual and as a learner. You are free to ask me these same questions if you like.

**Background:** Where did you grow up? What have you done in terms of school, extracurricular activities, jobs, and family life?

**Cultural Experience:** What experience have you had with cultures other than your own? People with backgrounds different from yours? What can be learned from such encounters? What did you learn from your encounters with people of other races or classes?

**Interests:** What do you like to do? What do you like to think and talk about?

**Achievements:** What achievements have given you the greatest personal satisfaction? Include things which gave you a real sense of accomplishment and pride, whether or not they're the sort of thing you'd list on a resume.

*What is your best method of learning?* Do you like to learn from books or do you prefer hands-on learning? Do you like to work alone or would you prefer to work with others when studying or doing a class project?

*What is your attitude toward reading?* Do you like to read? What do you read? Who is your favorite author? Book?

*What is your attitude toward writing?* Do you like to write? What writing experiences have you had in the past? Were they good ones? Include any school courses as well as work experience.

*How do you feel about this class?* Are you nervous? Confident? Explain your answer.

*Goals:* What do you hope to accomplish this quarter in terms of this class? Don't limit your answer to "a good grade." Think about it. What do you really want to learn from your experience in this class? What can I do to help you reach your goals?

Dr. Sue V. Lape
Columbus State Community College
Columbus, Oh

# Implementing the Electronic Classroom for Distance Education

There is little doubt that an electronic revolution is taking place in higher education. For more than a decade, videos, computers and other electronic media have been increasingly incorporated in coursework programs. Part-time adjunct faculty are part of the new wave of classroom leaders who are assisting adult learners in accessing new electronic information and using it to accomplish learning and educational goals. The schedules of working adults often make it impractical to travel to college campuses for coursework programs. Emerging as an important option to a growing and technologically skilled student population is distance education.

Distance education requires new skills and professional development from part-time adjunct instructors. The first hurdle to overcome is a change in professional direction and preparation. The electronic classroom is significantly different from the traditional classroom environment featuring an instructor engaged in a didactic lecture/discussion to a group of 20 or more students.

Adjunct faculty are now delivering instruction from telecommunications classrooms to adult students at distant learning sites. With few geographical limitations, students at various and remote locations are interacting with instructors through a televideo network and via computers. In this environment, there is less face-to-face interaction between teacher and student. What will instructors need in order to effectively communicate with students in the telecommunications classroom to ensure a suitable faculty/student relationship?

### 1. Learning New Information Technology

Faculty must fully embrace and learn how to appropriately include information technologies into every facet of the course. A dramatic pedagogical change requires new methodologies and the inclusion of new resources to facilitate teaching and learning. Part-time instructors must learn how to integrate video, text, image and audio clips into their courses. It is necessary to review current syllabi to determine how assignments can introduce and build student use of multimedia and electronic library resources, including the global Internet, to conduct research and analyze findings and turn in more current and content rich papers and projects.

A lesson plan, for example, includes specific activities using various sources of information: computer graphics and photos introduced to actively illustrate specific points; video clips to show field experiments or processes or capture an interview with an expert or specialist; formulas and computations with active, real-time student participation. Student and instructor activities are much more integrative as the course syllabus moves to increasingly more challenging academic content. In addition, a more explicit statement of course objectives is necessary and more substantive planning required for each class meeting.

### 2. New Instructional Methods

Creating a learning community between the instructor and distant and on-site learners requires faculty to develop new instructional methods. In-service training and feedback are essential for faculty to instruct in front of a camera, projecting a presence to the students at the distance learning site while attending to the needs of the students in the telecommunications classroom. Integrating audio-visual technology to replace traditional chalkboards and overhead projectors to display written material requires more skillful preparation. Effective communication skills are a must as the instructor remains the pivotal point in the delivery of specific academic content. In designing the course content, feedback is planned as part of the student activities, ensuring a level of connection with each participant. Obtaining this degree of information and interaction cannot be left to randomness; rather, the instructor must frame projects to incorporate production and class presentation. Specific goals and purposes are built into the course outline to expand the amount of feedback from an initial experience to a more sophisticated level.

### 3. Involving Students

When a current course is retooled for distance learning, new elements of classroom context and instructional design and development must be included. For example, student participation takes on a different role as they interact electronically in real time across distance with fellow students and the instructor. As the primary facilitator, the instructor must generate specific activities to encourage and promote multi-level discourse, dialogue and collaboration within the extended classroom. The design of a class bulletin board for discussion and sharing informational resources will require students to obtain an email account. Some courses utilize group email accounts for real time discussion of classroom topics during office hours. From this initial phase, the instructor will design an increasingly sophisticated sequence of activities for the students to interact electronically with each other and the instructor outside the teleclassroom.

For example, Class 300 will require each student to have an email address, either through the computing center or their own on-line connection. The bulletin board will be cl300@address, and students will be required to comment on weekly reading assignments, offer opinions, question the author and each other about the content, and prepare for class discussion and participation. Through the bulletin board, the instructor will forward information or articles from other sources to augment the weekly topic or show a new point of view. Students can also work on projects with each other over the bulletin board, coordinating research and reference searches and passing along findings. Groups or individuals can communicate with class members about what they are researching, ask for feedback and request if others find materials on a certain topic, to pass it along.

It is important to track student attitudes, academic achievement and course outcomes as the instructor moves through the content of the course. A fundamental question to assess is whether the course objectives are being met. Determining the level of student attention and measuring the effectiveness of new classroom techniques and technologies are critical pieces of information for the instructor to evaluate in reporting to academic departments and administrators. Assessment tools for a distance learning environment must examine not only classroom elements, but learning and informational resources as well.

As the "virtual university" becomes more of a reality, there is still a critical need for a valued and professional instructor. Embracing new technologies and gaining familiarity with distance learning classrooms is both exciting and challenging for part-time faculty members. Upgrading teaching skills will enhance the professionalism and academic standing of the part-time instructor who will play an important part in delivering education to a growing population of adult learners in the next millennia.

Harry Schuler, Ph. D.
A. Cathleen Greiner, M.A., M.S.
Chapman University
Orange, CA

# Use of Tests and/or Quizzes as Learning Experiences

Often students and perhaps some faculty consider testing to be only for the purpose of assigning grades. Such a limited view can lead to confusion in how to approach studying the course. Students may even feel that what is on the test is rather arbitrary.

Way back in an educational psychology course, my professor said to tell the students exactly what would be on the test and then to test on what you said would be tested. Simple, but it doesn't always work out that way.

With most textbooks showing objectives/competencies up front, this approach is easy. Be sure your own course objectives/competencies either match those of the text or make any variations clear to the student. With the first quiz, if the questions match your stated objectives/competencies for that unit, the students will catch on. In preparing for future tests students will know that the course objectives/competencies will be covered.

A corollary is that the weight of the concepts tested should be related to the emphasis placed on those concepts in course work through lectures, discussions, assignments, etc. Another obvious point, but it is often not followed in test construction.

Frequent short quizzes encourage students to keep up with the material. Feedback from those quizzes lets the teacher and the students know which concepts need more work.

Finally, even if you are using a published test with a prepared answer key, you should work through the test yourself. There are several advantages to doing this: you may discover the test is too long or too short, too easy or too difficult, not well balanced, contains confusing or wrong material, or can simply be improved. The students may also give you similar feedback either directly or indirectly after the test. That is a good time to jot down ideas for revision.

## Marking and Grading Assignments

Call it human nature or whatever, but students approach assignments with the same amount of seriousness as they perceive the teacher approaches the marking and grading of those assignments. During the first week or two, the honeymoon period, students usually make a serious effort on assignments. But, if those first papers are not handed back in a reasonable time or are marked in a perfunctory manner, most students will cut back considerably on the amount of effort put into assignments. By the end of term, that effort may be close to zero. While grading, in order to get full credit for the correct answer the students must show the work. It helps with consistency to grade all of one question at a time. I do not consider the grammar as part of the grade since I teach accounting, but I mark errors. Future student work shows more care in English usage.

The bottom line in getting students to produce high quality work is to set up the assignments with care and to spend the time marking the papers well. Once students are handed back papers with thoughtful feedback, they know your class is worth extra effort.

Jill Radcliffe
Ivy Tech State College
Bloomington, IN

# Periodical Review:
# Developing Research Skills in Basic Skills Readers

A primary goal of Basic Skills Reading courses is the development of sound reading habits that will, ultimately, result in text and in-class material mastery. Yet research is an inherent component of credit courses, and research requires not only sound reading habits, but also specific competencies in summarizing, paraphrasing, quoting, and citing. Related to sound reading practices, the written review of periodical literature provides a vehicle to apply identification of main idea, supporting details, and author's standpoint while simultaneously enhancing vocabulary and developing schemata. Why not incorporate appropriate summarizing, paraphrasing, quoting, and citing skills within this review format?

The enclosed review form evolved as the answer. Prior to each periodical reading, the instructor identifies and students then predefine new or troublesome vocabulary. Students then use these definitions to solve the reading and after reading, these become the concluding part of the review. Once the article is read, the students then start the formal review.

First, as proto-researchers they begin the review with appropriate bibliographic entry. Second, as readers they investigate the article by identifying and summarizing the main idea. Third, students separate and summarize salient details again at first recording these ideas in their own words and in proper sentence form. Fourth, students are called on to infer and then summarize the author's thesis, standpoint, objective, etc. in appropriate paragraph form. As proto-researchers, beginning students are required to summarize the reading using their own words, with severe penalties for plagiarism. The resultant review is a valid application of reading analysis and vocabulary expansion. But the review is also a working model of a valid, citable source using the legal-pad method of recording (facilitating later conversion to notecards). As a reader, the student has a review to submit to the Reading instructor that presents analytic and even inter-active thinking on the article concerned. And as a proto-researcher, the student has applied multiple research skills (highlighting, note-taking, summarizing). Further, the student leaves the Reading class with a working model as a reference for later research, and even has citable documents from each article studied that may be of use in later research assignments.

Predictably, I have found this procedure to be highly effective for both Developmental Reading and research project students. In addition to the skills already noted, this format for article dissection forces the research student to become involved in the article while categorizing information under the subtitles of main idea, supporting details, and author's opinion forces a logical outline of investigation. Complementarily, bibliographic entry, required orderly presentation, and later required quoting produce more competent work from basic skills students. The end result is a basic skills student, capable of approaching research material, whom I am secure in releasing to credit courses and whom it has been my pleasure to see walking into my Freshman English Composition course advantageously prepared to approach research assignments.

## Periodical Review Format

**Author's last name,  First name, Initial.** "Title of Article." Periodical Title. Day Month Year. Newspaper ed.: page number(s). **Main Idea.** (Summarize the main idea of this article in no more than two sentences and in your own words. With increasing competency, quotation and parenthetical citation can be added here and in Author's Opinion.)

**Details.** (Summarize in sentence form and in your own words, five important details that support and/or supply information for the main idea.)

    1.               4.

    2.               5.

    3.

(With developing competency, careful paraphrasing can be instructed and encouraged here, with reminders to record relevant, parenthetical page number or numbers.)

**Author's Opinion.** (In a paragraph explain whose side you think the author is on, whom or what he supports, etc.)

**Key Sentence.** (With developing competency, students can be instructed in recording and parenthetically citing a direct quotation. Here, students are instructed to cite a sentence that best summarizes the gist of the article.)

**Vocabulary.** (Instructor identifies troublesome words and students define these words prior to reading. Students are also encouraged to define any other words they do not know as these words may be included in the test on the article. All words are to be defined briefly and as they are relevant to the article and all words are to be numbered.)

Yvonne Collioud Sisko<br>
Middlesex County College<br>
Edison, NJ

# Easy Techniques for Outcomes Assessment

These are some of several techniques I have used that have been successful in determining how students are responding to the material presented. Through the feedback thus acquired, I can determine their needs and how I need to improve my teaching.

**1. Overcoming Syllabus Block**

My English students always seem to forget the syllabus moments after it is explained. Through their first-day panic, they seem to block out my carefully-defined goals, guidelines, requirements. To overcome this problem, I place the students in small groups (3 to 5) after presenting my syllabus. A Scribe is chosen to write down participant's comments about the syllabus in response to several questions:

1. What do you like most about what you are expected to do this semester?
2. What do you like least?
3. What points in the syllabus were not clear to you?
4. Is there any requirement that makes you especially apprehensive?

By getting a chance to look over the syllabus as a group and share their confusion and fears, the students consider the syllabus more carefully and feel more comfortable facing their apprehensions. Through their feedback, I can address the issues that are concerning them and find any weaknesses in the explanations provided in my syllabus.

### 2. Instant Assessment

Here's a quick and easy technique that can be used any time during the semester. I find the technique particularly useful when the class seems to be struggling but I'm not sure why. I simply distribute 3x5 cards and ask them to write down any questions, frustrations, or needs that they have. This technique gives them a chance to communicate with me anonymously about any problems they're having, any thing they need to have explained, or anything they just want to complain about. It is particularly effective with those students who are too reticent to ask questions. When I respond to the cards in class, the students know that their opinions and needs matter to me. And I find out what I need to teach more carefully.

### 3. Response Journals

I use response journals in Composition II where there are extensive reading assignments in essays, poetry and short stories. Most students are not used to reading literature with any depth and are sometimes overwhelmed by the apparent complexity of the literature we deal with. I ask them to write a one or two paragraph response to each reading assignment. The response is to include several sentences about what they felt was the main idea of the reading and several sentences of their reaction to the reading. I ask if there was any character, description, idea, etc. that they could identify with or that touched them or if there was any part that confused them.

These journals are handed in before we discuss the reading class. I then know what issues to address and what areas need to be clarified. I am frequently surprised to find out what they don't understand.

To make sure they put adequate effort into the assignment, I grade it loosely on the basis of one to four, four being the highest. With this method, I avoid the weightiness of letter grades. Their journal then counts as 10-20% of their final grade.

Jane C. Keller
Pennsylvania College of Technology
Williamsport, PA

# Strategies to Extend Student Thinking

* Call on students randomly, not just those with raised hands.
* Utilize "think-pair-share"

Two minutes of individual think time, two minutes of discussion with a partner, then open up the class discussion.

* Remember "wait time"

Ten to twenty seconds following a "higher level" question.

* Ask "follow-ups"

"Why?" "Do you agree?" "Can you elaborate?" "Tell me more." "Can you give an example?"

* Withhold judgment

Respond to student answers in a non-evaluative fashion.

* Ask for summary (to promote active listening)

"Could you please summarize John's point?"

* Survey the class

"How many people agree with the author's point of view?" ("thumbs up, thumbs down")

* Allow for student calling

"Susan, will you please call on someone else to respond?"

* Play devil's advocate

Require students to defend their reasoning against different points of view.

* Ask students to "unpack their thinking"

"Describe how you arrived at your answer." ("think aloud")

* Student questioning

Let the students develop their own questions.

* Cue student responses

"There is not a single correct answer for this question. I want you to consider alternatives."

Lynne McCauley
Western Michigan University
Kalamazoo, MI

# Teaching Seniors

As the population ages, more and more senior citizens are returning to school. As the instructor, it is vital that you take note of this and are responsive to the older population in your classroom. Below are some observations and suggestions for teaching seniors:

1. Find out why your students are taking the course. Someone who is there for job retraining may have different needs than a student who is there for companionship or personal growth.

2. Speak loudly and articulate carefully. Check in with your class every so often to make sure everyone can hear you. One of the biggest complaints among seniors is that they have trouble hearing the instructor, but often they are hesitant to make an issue of it.

3. Many seniors haven't been to school in awhile and can be overzealous learners. It helps to have good handouts with much of what you are saying on the printed page. This frees the students from taking volumes of notes, helps the student who has trouble hearing, and is comforting to the nervous student.

4. Ask for life-experiences from the students, and include stories and anecdotes from your own life in your lectures. Get to know the people in your classes, and call them by their names.

5. Provide regular breaks for classes that meet for more than an hour at a time.

Carol Cohen
Lakeland Community College
Mentor, OH

## Ways To Elicit Feedback

The following are several specific techniques for eliciting feedback about teaching from students:

1. The One Minute Paper: During the last few minutes of class, ask students to respond to these two questions on a sheet of paper which they can turn in on their way out of class: a) What was the most useful/meaningful thing you learned during this session, and b) What question(s) remain(s) upper-most in your mind as we end this session?

2. After taking a test, encourage students to be aware of their responsibility by asking this question: "What could you have done to better prepare for this test?" And after group exercises asking: a) "What did you contribute to the learning of your group members today," and b) "How have you applied this material in your personal life?"

3. Ask students to help you solve the problems that arise in designing the course. Suggestions provide you with valuable input and give students a sense of ownership.

4. To elicit feedback from students who perform poorly on a quiz/test, ask the following questions: a) "Was the written information clear (if not, why?)" b) "How could the instructor have been

clearer in class about the answers," and c) "What could you have done to better prepare for this quiz/test?"

Donna K. Kirkley
Howard Community College
Columbia, MD

## Eight Principles to Observe When Developing A Grading Plan

One area that frequently raises conflict between students and teachers is misunderstanding concerning grades. James Hammons and Janice Barnsley provide suggestions for clarification of grading principles to avoid misunderstanding.

**Principle #1:  Communicate the grading system in writing.** Include as a minimum what will be measured, the weight attached to it, and a timetable of due dates.

**Principle #2:  Measure a variety of behaviors.** Include outside assignments, projects, activities etc., not just knowledge.

**Principle #3:  Provide prompt feedback.** In addition to the traditional methods, give "quality circles" a try.

**Principle #4:  Evaluate on different levels.** Blooms taxonomy is a good start. If you haven't used it, look it up.

**Principle #5:  Weigh types of performance according to importance.** Assign different weights to different evaluation activities.

**Principle #6:  Be creative in evaluating student performance.** Don't get in a rut. Use different grading systems for different courses.

**Principle #7:  Match evaluation measurements to course activities and objectives.** Too often faculty are accused of teaching or lecturing on one subject and grading on another.

**Principle #8:  Decide on retest possibilities.** This becomes difficult because of the fairness to students who had only one chance. Some issues to consider:  the determination of mastery, the number of points for scoring above the satisfactory level on subsequent tries, the number of times the student is allowed to try.

Hammons, J.O., & Barnsley, J.R. (1992)
***Journal On Excellence in College Teaching 3***, 1992
Miami University, Oxford, OH

## Improving Classroom Communication

Most authorities agree that good communication in the classroom is a prerequisite to learning. Foremost in the communication process is the ability of the instructor to exemplify good communication by utilizing an effective speaking style. Listed below are several ideas to improve classroom speaking.

* Speak loudly, clearly, and at a rate comfortable to you.
* Avoid attaching yourself to the lectern, it should be used to hold notes, not as a crutch. Above all do not sit at the desk.
* Keep your eyes on the students. Look for non-verbal as well as verbal feedback.
* Never read lectures.
* Speak from an outline, rather than a script.
* Use supplements (charts, graphs, overheads) for explanations whenever possible.
* Encourage a friendly open atmosphere. Try to monitor understanding. Rather than saying, "everybody got that?", ask a student to rephrase the idea or concept.
* Move around the classroom. Moving close to the students indicates openness and friendliness.
* Present yourself energetically and with confidence. Audiences will invest about as much confidence in the speaker as the speaker demands.
* Allow disagreement without being defensive.
* Enter the classroom with optimism and good will. Some instructors introduce themselves to the students individually as they arrive for the first class.

Janice Peterson
Santa Barbara City College
Santa Barbara, CA

## Establishing Educational Objectives

Perhaps, one of the most crucial elements of any classroom is to establish a long range (semester) focus for both the students and the faculty member. This needs to be initiated with the first class. Since I teach a composition course, I use several practical but revealing questions. These can be modified to adapt to any classroom.

1. Why are you here at college?
2. What do you expect to learn from this class? What is your objective?
3. What do you plan to do to achieve your objective?
4. What was the best book, short story, or article you ever read? Why?
5. What was the last book you read?

Then on the reverse side of this paper I have the students introduce themselves to me. They are to do a multi-paragraph written introduction.

After these are collected, I use them for discussion. As the students offer their perceptions, I can provide the semester's objectives and my expectations. Likewise, these serve as excellent diagnostic tools in that I return them at the end of the semester at which time the students have the opportunity to discover the improvement in their writing styles—the major goal of my course.

## Practical Classroom Suggestions

Essentially, the success of any classroom is enhanced by the three "E's." First, the instructor needs to exhibit ENTHUSIASM in the teaching and in the approach to the subject matter. Enthusiasm is contagious and breeds students' EXCITEMENT for this class. If both are working, the result is a dynamic EDUCATION.

To achieve this success, the instructor must be well prepared for each and every class. He or she should begin and end each class on time. All homework papers need to be evaluated with a clear educational objective for each. All evaluated materials should be passed back to the students on a timely basis—homework, next class and major products, no longer than a week. Above all the instructor must encourage, motivate, stimulate, and challenge the students. He or she should avoid yes or no questions but use those that provoke *thinking*. He or she is a facilitator of learning—the most precious part of the students' existence.

Bob Lebda
PA College of Technology
Williamsport, PA.

# Improving Timeliness of Student Reading with "Hot Chalk"

When all students have read their assigned material, the quality of class discussion improves. However, getting all students to do their reading in a timely manner and dissuading them from waiting until just before the test can prove challenging.

"Hot Chalk" begins at the start of class early in the semester and initially targets the back row of students in an Instructional Techniques class for prospective two-year college teachers. The "game" begins when the chalk is handed to a student who must answer a question about the assigned reading. If stumped, the rules allow the student to pass-the-chalk to another student but **NOT** back to the instructor. Satisfactory answers also require the student to pass-the-chalk to another student for the next question. Each student may answer only one question during a class meeting and the instructor must ask for the chalk back when finished.

"Hot Chalk" works. The prospect of receiving the chalk, combined with responsibility to the class and not just the instructor, has been a successful motivator to move students to do their reading on time. For students accustomed to letting the verbal, always prepared students do all the talking in class, "Hot Chalk" can be initially intimidating. Skill in rewarding wrong answers and making a joke of having to pass-the-chalk when a student is unprepared are keys to making the game work.

Surprisingly, the end of the semester student course evaluations are consistently peppered with positive comments about "Hot Chalk." Rarely has any student objected to the practice. The reputation for the game has spread among incoming students as evidenced by fewer averted eyes at the first offering of the "Hot Chalk." It also has done much to lessen the popularity of the back row!

Bill Frye, Ph.D.
The University of Akron
Akron, OH

# References

Bloom, B. S., et al., *Taxonomy of Educational Objectives*, New York: David McKay Co., 1956.

Frye, Bill J., et. al., *Teaching in College-A Resource For College Teachers*, Cleveland: Info-Tec, Inc., 1994.

Kazmierski, Paul R., "Learning Styles", *Teaching and Learning for Careers*, 1977, 2 (2) 1.

Knowles, Malcolm, *The Adult Learner-A Neglected Species*, Houston TX, Gulf Publishing Co., 1990.

Mager, Robert F., *Preparing Instructional Objectives*, Belmont, CA: Fearon Publishers, 1962.

McCarthy, Bernice, *The 4MAT System*, Barrington, IL: Excel Inc., 1987.

McKeachie, Wilbert J., et al., *Teaching Tips*, Lexington MA: D. C. Heath and Co., 1994.

Sego, Arlene, *Cooperative Learning-A Classroom Guide*, Cleveland OH: Info-Tec Inc., 1991.

Weimer, Maryellen, *Improving College Teaching*, San Francisco: Jossey-Bass, 1990.

## OTHER TEACHING SUPPORT PUBLICATIONS
## FROM INFO-TEC INC.

Teaching In College-A Resource for College Teachers     $24.95

Teaching Strategies For Adjunct Faculty     5.95

Total Quality Education-Teaching Techniques for
    Technical Educators     5.95

Cooperative Learning-A Classroom Guide     5.95

Non-Credit Instruction: A Guide for Continuing
    and Adult Education Programs     5.95

Bookmarks-Teaching Tips (Set of Three)     1.00

## To Order

**Info-Tec Inc.**
**1005 North Abbe Road**
**Elyria, OH 44035-1691**
**1-800-995-5222  x4632   ✦   Fax: 1-216-365-6519**